Richard Nelson's plays include *Two Shakespearean Actors* (Royal Shakespeare Company, Lincoln Center Theatre, N.Y.), *Some Americans Abroad* (RSC, Lincoln Center Theatre), *Sensibility and Sense* (American Playhouse), *Principia Scriptoriae* (RSC, Manhattan Theatre Club), *Between East and West* (Hampstead Theatre Club, Yale Repertory Theatre), *The Return of Pinocchio*, *Rip Van Winkle or The Works*, *The Vienna Notes* and *An American Comedy*. Radio plays include *Languages Spoken Here* (BBC Radio 3), *Eating Words* (Radio 4 and the World Service), *Roots in Water* (Radio 3), and *Advice to Eastern Europe*.

Among his awards are the prestigious Lila Wallace–Reader's Digest Award in 1991, a London *Time Out* Award, two Obies, two Giles Cooper Awards, a Guggenheim Fellowship, two Rockefeller playwriting grants and two National Endowment for the Arts playwriting fellowships.

by the same author

SENSIBILITY AND SENSE
SOME AMERICANS ABROAD
TWO SHAKESPEAREAN ACTORS
PRINCIPIA SCRIPTORIAE and
BETWEEN EAST AND WEST

COLUMBUS AND THE DISCOVERY OF JAPAN

Richard Nelson

faber and faber
LONDON · BOSTON

First published in 1992 by
Faber and Faber Limited
3 Queen Square London WC1N 3AU

Photoset by Parker Typesetting Service, Leicester
Printed by Clays Ltd, St Ives plc

A CIP record for this book is available from the British Library

ISBN 0–571–16857–4

T 1000630959

2 4 6 8 10 9 7 5 3 1

For Cynthia

CHARACTERS

(The position held on the voyage is in parenthesis.)

CHRISTOPHER COLUMBUS, early forties (Admiral of the fleet and Captain of the *Santa Maria*)
BEATRICE, twenty-five, his mistress
DIEGO, eleven, his son

In Seville
RODRIGO PULGAR, early forties, a wealthy landowner (Secretary of the fleet, sailed on the *Santa Maria*)
MIGUEL GARCÍA, fifties ⎫
PERO DE SORIA, fifties ⎭ friends of Pulgar's father
JUAN DE LA ENZINA, thirties, a poet
PEDRO DE TERREROS, twenties (Columbus's steward on the *Santa Maria*)

In Palos
MARTÍN ALONSO PINZÓN, fifty (Captain of the *Pinta*)
VINCENTE PINZÓN, thirty-two, his brother (Captain of the *Niña*)
FRANCISCO PINZÓN, his brother (Master of the *Pinta*)
FELIPA PINZÓN, fifty, wife of Martín
FATHER JUAN PEREZ, head of the friary La Rabida
CRISTOBAL QUINTEROS, late forties (owner of the *Pinta*)
JUAN NIÑOS, forties (owner and Master of the *Niña*)
LUIS DE TORRES (translator for the fleet)
Other OFFICERS, SAILORS and a CAULKER

In Cadiz
DIEGO DE HARANA, forties, Beatrice's cousin (Master-at-arms of the fleet, sailed on the *Santa Maria*)
JUAN SANCHEZ, forties, Beatrice's cousin (Surgeon of the *Santa Maria*)

Workers, servants, players, a man at the inn, a boy, Arawak Indians and others. (An extra group of actors are needed to represent the crews of the *Pinta*, *Niña* and the *Santa Maria* in Act Three, and to play the scenes which are seen through doors and windows in Acts One and Two.)

Columbus and the Discovery of Japan was first performed at the Barbican Theatre, London, on 22 July 1992. The cast was as follows:

CHRISTOPHER COLUMBUS	Jonathan Hyde
BEATRICE	Jane Gurnett
DIEGO	Simon Magnus/Luke Nugent
RODRIGO PULGAR	Philip Voss
MIGUEL GARCÍA	Bernard Gallagher
PERO DE SORIA	Michael Poole
JUAN DE LA ENZINA	Michael Higgs
PEDRO DE TERREROS	Christopher Luscombe
MARTÍN ALONSO PINZÓN	Christopher Benjamin
VINCENTE PINZÓN	Don Gallagher
FRANCISCO PINZÓN	Tim Hudson
FELIPA PINZÓN	Helen Blatch
FATHER JUAN PEREZ	Terence Wilton
CRISTOBAL QUINTEROS	Christopher Saul
JUAN NIÑOS	Howard Crossley
LUIS DE TORRES	David Birrell
DIEGO DE HARANA	Robert Domeger
JUAN SANCHEZ	Albie Woodington
CABIN BOY	Daniel Robson/Robbie Gill

Sailors, players, courtiers, villagers, servants and Arawak Indians played by David Birrell, Constance Byrne, Oliver Darley, Ian Hartley, Michael Higgs, Andrew McDonald, Stephen Moyer, Nick Simons and Biddy Wells.

Director	John Caird
Set Designer	Timothy O'Brien
Costume Designer	Jenny Jones
Lighting Designer	David Hersey
Music	Shaun Davey
Sound	Steff Langley and Monkey
Music Director	Richard Brown
Dialect Coach	Jill McCullough
Assistant Director	Colin Ellwood
Company voice work	Andrew Wade and Barbara Houseman
Stage Manager	Eric Lumsden
Deputy Stage Manager	Martin Christopher
Assistant Stage Managers	Deborah Gibbs and Lynda Snowden

AUTHOR'S NOTE

This play is based on many, but not all, of the facts known today about Christopher Columbus and his first voyage across the Ocean Sea in 1492.

I wish to thank the Lila Wallace–Reader's Digest Fund for its support during the writing of this play.

ACT ONE

SCENE I

Projection: SEVILLE, AUTUMN 1491

1a

A small transient apartment which overlooks the courtyard of an inn.
Sunset.

  A door to a hall, a bed, a chair, and a window through which is heard
a crowd laughing, cheering and applauding the performance of a farce
with songs, an 'auto' which is being performed in the courtyard below.
(The play concerns a man who is tricked into marrying his own
daughter, though little of the play can be understood at this distance –
mostly just the odd shouted line and the audience's reactions and a bit of
song.) The farce plays throughout the scene.

  COLUMBUS *sits on the bed, pulling on his trousers.* BEATRICE,
twenty-five, leans out of the window, watching the farce below; she is
half-undressed and with a towel wipes her thighs and between her legs
after sex.

  A burst of laughter from the crowd.

COLUMBUS: Who are they laughing at now?

BEATRICE: The old man. He's marrying his daughter. (*Turning to*
    COLUMBUS.) He doesn't know it's his –

COLUMBUS: I didn't think . . .

BEATRICE: (*Continues to clean herself*) She has a veil on. But the
    priest – isn't a real priest.

COLUMBUS: (*To himself*) What a surprise.

BEATRICE: He's her –

COLUMBUS: Lover.

BEATRICE: How did you – ?

COLUMBUS: Just lucky.

    (*He stands; another burst of laughter.*)

BEATRICE: (*Holding out the towel*) Here, don't you need to – ?
    (*She throws him the towel, as yet another burst of laughter occurs.*
    This turns into song: 'Oy comamos'. COLUMBUS *sticks the towel*
    into his trousers and cleans himself. BEATRICE *has turned back to*
    the courtyard and begins to smile, enjoying the farce very much.

I

COLUMBUS *watches her as she begins to giggle, then giggle more, and finally she bursts out laughing.*)

COLUMBUS: (*Unable to control himself*) Stop it!!! (*He throws down the towel.*) How can you laugh at that? He writes rubbish! That is rubbish!

BEATRICE: (*Stunned*) It's – .

COLUMBUS: It's what they want so – he writes it! He was a poet. Juan was an excellent poet.

BEATRICE: He can still – .

COLUMBUS: Not when you start to write – .

BEATRICE: (*Fighting back*) They're having a good time; what is so wrong with giving people a good – ?!

COLUMBUS: (*Over this*) I thought you were a smart woman! And then I watch you – ! You look like a horse, laughing like a – !

BEATRICE: Why are you saying this?!
(*Beat. They catch their breath.*)
Five minutes ago . . . (*She gestures towards their bed.*)

COLUMBUS: I knew Juan. He was a student. We have been friends. We've spent – evening after evening after . . . I just hate to see him . . .

BEATRICE: Make money?

COLUMBUS: (*Nodding towards the door*) Perhaps you'd like me to fetch Juan. It sounds like you and he – !

BEATRICE: Get him!! Get him!!
(*This irrational argument pauses.*)
(*Breathing heavily*) What have I done?
(*From the courtyard a character in the play cries:* 'Help me! Help me!' *More laughter.*)

COLUMBUS: (*Shakes his head*) I don't know. (*Shrugs.*) I beg your pardon. (*Beat.*) I beg. I beg. That is what I do best. Either you have something, which you sell . . . (*Gestures towards the window.*) Or you beg. (*Reaches into his pocket to take out money.*) You have poems, you have talent, you have – dreams. You sell them. Or you beg. (*Sets coins on the table.*)

BEATRICE: We were celebrating. For two months you've been saying – when Señor Pulgar gives you money . . . This will be the sign that he may – will – support the voyage. Today you have that sign. He gave you money!

2

COLUMBUS: Seven ducats.

BEATRICE: Is a sign! This is money! We can eat! If he didn't have plans, then he wouldn't be wasting his money. Even seven – .

COLUMBUS: I said to myself, this is going to be my day! (*Laughs.*) I said, before asking for the money – he'd waited me out, by the way; I'd thought I wouldn't have to *ask*! I hinted, I thought quite well, he seems to take the hint, it all seemed – . But I had to ask. (*Beat.*) So I said to myself – eight ducats. Accept nothing less. And this is where I draw the line. Anything less and he's not – he's not serious, is he? The line . . . (*Beat.*) So he immediately gives me – *seven* ducats. And – I redraw the line. For one ducat, I tell myself – you can't throw away all the time you've spent here in Seville, with Pulgar. He hands me seven!! I see seven!!!
(*He is half laughing and half crying. Pause. Music is now played off in the courtyard.*)

BEATRICE: (*At the window*) They're dancing. Come and take a – .

COLUMBUS: (*Ignoring her*) You must know when to quit. You trust yourself that you will know it when the time comes. Like one knows underwater when to go back to the surface and breathe. (*Beat.*) I trust I will know this. My body will tell me this. Someone will tell me – . Please, God, tell me.

BEATRICE: Seven ducats seems a lot to me. I would be flattered. He must like you. If someone gave me – .
(*Three loud bangs on the door. They look at each other.*)

COLUMBUS: How much do we owe?
(BEATRICE *shrugs.* COLUMBUS *straightens himself as he goes to answer the door, putting on his 'public' face of confidence. He opens the door. A* BOY *is there.*)

BOY: Señor Columbus?
(COLUMBUS *nods. The* BOY *hands him a letter.*)

COLUMBUS: (*As he opens the letter*) Just a minute, let me give you something. (*He looks in his pockets, looks around then goes back to the table where the seven ducats are, all the time reading the note.*)

BEATRICE: Christopher, that's much too much to give – !

COLUMBUS: Stop it!

3

(*He gives the* BOY *a ducat. The* BOY *is stunned by his good fortune, nods happily, unable even to speak, and then hurries off, almost running into the door.*)

COLUMBUS: Did you see that boy's face?

(*He closes the door and smiles.*) He nearly – right into the door. He must have walked in here and thought – that we were – that we're nothing. You look at this room and you think – . But then he gets a ducat. He gets a whole ducat! (*Laughs.*) He'll talk about this for days. I'll be famous on his street! (*He laughs, puts the letter down and begins to straighten his hair and clothes. Outside, the dance is just finishing.*) Señor Pulgar has invited me to dinner. (*Beat.*) Someone couldn't come.

(*Huge applause outside for the end of the dance and the play.*)

1b

Room in Rodrigo Pulgar's home. Evening. A table, chairs, and a door to the entrance hall. Around the table are COLUMBUS, PULGAR, *a wealthy Jewish landowner, and two older wealthy friends who are visiting,* MIGUEL GARCÍA *and* PERO DE SORIA. *Food is on the table; the middle of a conversation.*

SORIA: In the street?

COLUMBUS: They seem to set up – . Put up benches, then a platform and there they are. They'd taken over the courtyard of the inn. When I left – tens of people, peasants mostly, how they heard about it – . I suppose they just hear the music and . . . (*Shrugs.*)

SORIA: Fascinating.

PULGAR: Isn't it?

GARCÍA: I've never heard of anything like it. Was there some sort of story?

COLUMBUS: The old one about a father who marries his daughter. Nothing even original.

SORIA: I don't think I know that one.

GARCÍA: I don't either.

(COLUMBUS *smiles, disbelieving.*)

COLUMBUS: There's the priest – who isn't a priest, of course. He's the one who marries them.

4

SORIA: How can he marry if – ?

COLUMBUS: He doesn't really.

SORIA: But I thought the father – .

COLUMBUS: He thinks he is marrying, but – . He doesn't know
it's his daughter, by the way. That's not the – .

GARCÍA: He doesn't know his own – ?

COLUMBUS: She's disguised. The priest – well, I'm sure you
know who that turns out to be. You've read . . .
(*They look at him; obviously they don't know.*)
The priest is really the girl's – .

GARCÍA: (*Guessing*) Brother!

COLUMBUS: Lover!

GARCÍA: Oh. (*Turns to Soria.*) I would never have guessed that.

SORIA: Me neither.

COLUMBUS: It's a rather common . . .
(*He turns to* PULGAR, *who is trying not to smile.*)

SORIA: To have a priest as your lover? I think I have been
spending too much time in the country.
(*He laughs.* GARCÍA *laughs at this.*)

COLUMBUS: (*Getting frustrated*) He isn't – !
(*They stop laughing and turn to* COLUMBUS.)
He isn't a – a priest.

SORIA: But you said – .

COLUMBUS: (*With too much force*) You weren't listening!!
(*An awkward moment as* SORIA *and* GARCÍA *glance at*
PULGAR.)
Or perhaps I wasn't being clear.

PULGAR: (*To* SORIA *and* GARCÍA) Juan de la Enzina's a poet of
some achievement.

COLUMBUS: This is true, but – .

PULGAR: (*Ignoring him*) I have read some of his verse.

COLUMBUS: That's why – . To see him, a man with his talents,
writing this rubbish, putting it on in the streets, for peasants,
I – .

PULGAR: (*Over this*) Señor Enzina was to join us tonight.

GARCÍA: Ohhh, I – .

SORIA: (*At the same time*) That would have been very – .

COLUMBUS: (*Interrupting*) I didn't realize you know – Enzina. We

5

were together at Salamanca. While he was a – student.
(*Beat.*) I know him. I'm sorry he won't be coming. At least
you have me. (*Laughs.*) Anyway, we were talking about – the
– getting the attention of the court and seeking its
permission. For the voyage. Our voyage. I assume this is
why Señor Pulgar wished me to meet . . . Wished us to – .
(*Smiles.*) Sometimes – . (*Reaches for more wine.*)
Anyone want more wine?
(*They shake their heads and he pours some for himself.*)
Sometimes it's really as if I have already taken this journey.
That I have already been there. Amazing, isn't it. To feel, to
have it – that tangible. That – immediate. And to be – that
confident. Ask our host – have I not spoken a hundred times
as if this voyage had already taken place? Or at least as if it
were a complete certainty?
PULGAR: Señor Columbus, let us have our turn at speaking for a
while.
(*An embarrassed moment. A servant pours wine for the others;*
COLUMBUS *hesitates, then nods and drinks.*)
SORIA: It's a pity the poet couldn't join us. (*Beat. To* COLUMBUS)
I didn't mean – . I would have liked to have met you both.
GARCÍA: (*While chewing, to* PULGAR) I've built a new set of
rooms. I haven't told you?
PULGAR: You have, but tell me again.
(*He laughs, as do the others, except for* COLUMBUS.)
GARCÍA: It was a very good harvest.
PULGAR: I think it was for all of us.
(GARCÍA *turns to* COLUMBUS.)
COLUMBUS: I don't have any land.
SORIA: (*To* PULGAR) You heard about Andres? I've told you
about him?
PULGAR: Andres??
SORIA: My sister's boy, Andres. You remember. When you
visited.
PULGAR: With the slippers! When I couldn't find my – .
SORIA: That's another Andres. There were two in the house.
That was a cousin. My aunt's daughter's Andres. (*Beat.*)
Blond hair? About this tall?

6

PULGAR: I don't remember the blond hair. With a little scar?

SORIA: Scar? Who has a scar? That's Carlos! Andres, my sister's Andres, he – . Maybe he wasn't even born yet when you were there. Now that I think of it, he – . When were you there?

PULGAR: The last time?

SORIA: You've only visited the one time, Rodrigo.

PULGAR: Didn't my uncle – ?

SORIA: I mean as an adult. You've visited us only once as an adult. And that is not my fault.

PULGAR: You have graciously offered – .

GARCÍA: When did he visit ?!

PULGAR: (*Shrugs*) Four years ago?

GARCÍA: And when was Andres born? Your sister's Andres.

SORIA: (*Shrugs*) Three years ago.

GARCÍA: Then he hasn't met him.

SORIA: I suppose not.

(*Pause. They eat.*)

GARCÍA: So – ? What about Andres? You started to say – .

SORIA: Oh. (*Finishes chewing, wipes his mouth.*) He – . He died.

(*The others nod their sympathies.*)

It was during the harvest. We were talking about the harvest.

(*The others nod.*)

I suppose that was rather boring.

(*The others shake their heads, but of course it was.*)

(*Turns to* COLUMBUS) Rodrigo says you're from Genoa.

Funny, I don't hear the accent.

COLUMBUS: I've lived away for – .

SORIA: (*To the others*) Wonderful city, Genoa. I go there whenever I can. I go there on my way to Milan.

GARCÍA: Speaking of Milan. I was having dinner with someone last week. Guillermo – . I forget his name.

SORIA: Guillermo? I know two – .

GARCÍA: And he'd been to Milan – or he knew someone who had recently been to Milan – the man who's there, what's his name? He saw some of his drawings.

PULGAR: Who saw – ??

GARCÍA: There's an artist – a draughtsman there – and, this man, he seems to take corpses, cut them up and – you remember details like these – pours water over the cuts to flush the blood out, then, with extraordinary detail, draws – I don't know. Pieces. What he saw was a thigh.

PULGAR: In Milan?

SORIA: (*At the same time*) Does he sell these? Are they worth anything?

GARCÍA: (*Shrugs*) It does seem – I don't know. They say he's a brilliant draughtsman. But to sit with dead rotting bodies and the flies and – . And try and draw – .

COLUMBUS: I admire it myself.

GARCÍA: (*Continuing*) You have to wonder – .

COLUMBUS: The will it takes to – see past the stench, the flies, and see – .

GARCÍA: (*To the others*) I suppose I'm not an artist.

COLUMBUS: Neither am I, but – .

GARCÍA: I know this. You are a secretary.

COLUMBUS: Secretary? Where did you – ? (*Turns to* PULGAR.)

PULGAR: Señor Columbus has been doing a few letters and whatever for me. Excellent, Miguel.

GARCÍA: Latin?

COLUMBUS: Excuse me?

GARCÍA: (*Over this*) Do you know Latin?

COLUMBUS: Yes, but – .

PULGAR: Señor García is in need of a secretary. He asked if I knew of someone.

GARCÍA: When you mentioned Genoa, I was afraid of the accent, but he's – .

PULGAR: As I told you.

GARCÍA: (*Turns to* COLUMBUS) I do too much work at the court to have a secretary with an accent. And with the war ending – .

SORIA: Do you think that will be good or bad?

GARCÍA: For us Jews? We should talk about just that. Later. (*Turns to* COLUMBUS.) If my friend says you are a good secretary – .

COLUMBUS: I am not looking to become someone's secretary! I'd hoped I was asked here to discuss getting financing for – .

PULGAR: He's a map-maker right now.

GARCÍA: You told me. I'd like to see – . We were just speaking of draughtsmen – .

PULGAR: He has a map. Quite attractive. And the story of how he came to make it – . There was an ancient pilot, correct? He comes into Columbus's home. He'd been lost in a storm at sea – and he chooses Columbus to – . Why did he choose your house?

COLUMBUS: I don't know, I suppose he just happened to be – .

PULGAR: And he tells Columbus of the islands across the Ocean Sea. Is that right? Or a route, he says – .

COLUMBUS: Which he drew up. And I have – clarified in my map.

PULGAR: As I said – a map-maker.

COLUMBUS: And for seven months – . For seven months Señor Pulgar and I have been discussing his support – .

PULGAR: Christopher – .

COLUMBUS: Seven months. Time enough, one would think, to make up his mind. Perhaps I should just give up on him and find someone else who's a little more excited about supporting such an enterprise – more interested in the immense profits to be gained. Is that what you'd like me to do, Señor Pulgar? (*Smiles.*)

PULGAR: Our friend has even presented his plan to the court. When was this? A few years ago. For a trade route to – ? China? Japan? Across the Ocean Sea. I'm sure they were highly entertained. He's never actually captained a ship. Though he's travelled – .

COLUMBUS: I have the calculations – .

PULGAR: Contradicted by eminent scholars.

COLUMBUS: A fact I have never hidden. If one only listened to scholars, where would we be?

PULGAR: He's a very good – talker!

COLUMBUS: It's not just the map! I know this journey is possible! And if we don't – then – . The ancient pilot, he also mentioned seeing boats – native boats . . .

PULGAR: From – ?

COLUMBUS: China! Japan! He saw huge boats. It'll just be a

matter of time before they sail to – .

PULGAR: This is the first I've heard of this.

COLUMBUS: Didn't I mention – ? It must have slipped my mind. I thought I'd convinced you. After seven months, I thought – !!

PULGAR: (*Interrupting, to* GARCÍA) He shall make an excellent secretary. I can assure you of this.

GARCÍA: I can see we are bargaining. I shall have to begin by saying I do not need a secretary! (*Laughs.*)

COLUMBUS: I cannot consider anything, while we are still discussing the voyage.

PULGAR: Then we should stop discussing it.
(*The noise of a crowd of people arriving – from the hallway. A servant opens the door and the noise is very loud. The servant goes to* PULGAR, *whispers to him and hands him a note.*)

PULGAR: (*Getting up*) It seems our poet could come after all. And he's brought along some of his players.
(*Music is heard from the hallway.*)
(*To* GARCÍA *and* SORIA) Come, let me introduce you.
(*The crowd of players can be seen through the doorway.* PULGAR *begins to lead* GARCÍA *and* SORIA *out, looking at the note.*)
(*With the note*) Señor Enzina has written a poem in my honour. And he wishes to recite it.
(GARCÍA *and* SORIA *nod and applaud lightly. Suddenly a masked player bursts into the room.*)
(*Turning him around*) This way. This way. There'll be food out here.
(*They go, leaving* COLUMBUS *alone with a servant, who begins to clean up. From the hallway, music and laughter – a few players have begun a song. Another* SERVANT *enters.*)

SERVANT: (*To* FIRST SERVANT) Señor Pulgar needs the seven ducats for the poet.

COLUMBUS: (*To* FIRST SERVANT, *who takes out a purse*) Seven – ducats?? Why seven?
(*Beat.*)

FIRST SERVANT: It's what he always pays to the entertainers.
(*A huge laugh from the hallway – the entertainment is being enjoyed.*)

The stairs (through a trap) and hallway outside Columbus's transient apartment. Night. A full moon, and shafts of light from the windows.

COLUMBUS *struggles up the stairs; he is drunk. He is supported by a young man in his late teens or early twenties –* PEDRO DE TERREROS. *The door to the apartment is closed and bolted from the inside.*

COLUMBUS: (*Coming up the stairs*) I have decided to give it all back to him. Just give it back to – . Did I say this already? I shall give – . All of it. (*He is taking out his purse.*) Whatever's – left I'll – . (*Counts the change.*) Three ducats. About three . . . (*Turns on* PEDRO.) What happened to the – ! (*Stops himself.*) All of it, back to Senõr Rodrigo Pulgar! Take it! (*He throws the money up in the air.* PEDRO *scrambles to pick it up on the stairs.* COLUMBUS *laughs.*)
I am no flatterer, no enter – . I can't be bought for . . . (*He slips,* PEDRO *hurries to him.*)

PEDRO: Careful! (*He holds* COLUMBUS *up.*) Which room is it? (COLUMBUS *nods toward the door.*)

COLUMBUS: You come with me and watch. Pulgar! Watch his face when I . . .
(*He looks at* PEDRO, *swallows hard, tries to focus his eyes.*)
It's not because he's a Jew. Pulgar. I like Jews. (*Leans on the railing.*) I don't like Moors. Who else don't I like? I don't like Venetians. Marco Polo felt the same way and he was a Venetian. I don't like . . . (*Beat.*) No – Jews are – . (*Shrugs.*)
He said he was my friend. You heard him say this!

PEDRO: I wasn't there.
(PEDRO *leans down and picks up another thrown coin.*)

COLUMBUS: He said . . .
(PEDRO *tries the door. It is locked. He knocks.*)
Seven wasted months!
(*Suddenly and with tremendous violence,* COLUMBUS *rams his head against a pillar.* PEDRO *is stunned; he knocks harder, as he is panicked now. Blood pours down* COLUMBUS's *face. Voices from rooms below can be heard shouting for the noise to stop.*)

PEDRO: (*As he knocks*) Why did you do . . . ?! Hello! Hello!

(*The door opens;* BEATRICE *is there. She looks at* PEDRO, *then hears* COLUMBUS *whining in pain.*)

BEATRICE: Oh God. What is – ?! Christopher!!
(*Goes to him.*)
Get him here! Here, put your arm . . . Lift him up.

PEDRO: (*At the same time*) We met in the – . He threw his head against – !

BEATRICE: Thank you! I have him.

COLUMBUS: I am not a secretary!!!!

BEATRICE: (*Taking* COLUMBUS *into the room*) I've never seen you drink like this.
(*They are gone – though what takes place in the room can be seen and heard, somewhat, through the doorway.*
PEDRO *is alone in the hallway. He sees another coin, bends down and picks it up. From below, the neighbours shout for the noise to stop.*
BEATRICE *returns to the door.*)

BEATRICE: (*To* PEDRO) Does he owe you money? We don't have any money. (*She starts to close the door.*)

PEDRO: I met him at the inn – .
(*As* BEATRICE *closes the door, she sees something behind her that terrifies her.*)

BEATRICE: Christopher, don't!!! Get away from the window!!!
(*From inside, a chair is turned over as* BEATRICE *struggles to pull* COLUMBUS *away from the window.*
PEDRO *pushes gently at the door, and it swings open.* BEATRICE *suddenly appears at the door and* PEDRO *jumps back.*)
We'll pay. Whatever he owes! Tomorrow, come back – .

PEDRO: (*Holding out the coins*) He left these.
(*Beat.* BEATRICE *looks at* PEDRO, *then back into the room. Then, instead of taking the coins, she folds* PEDRO's *hand over them.*)
Nearly three ducats.

BEATRICE: We need two horses and provisions. Two horses, do you understand? Can I trust you?

PEDRO: (*Opens his hand*) I could have taken – .

BEATRICE: He had *six* ducats when he left here!

PEDRO: (*Defending himself*) He must have spent – !

12

BEATRICE: (*Interrupting*) I trust you! I can't go myself . . .
  (COLUMBUS *has begun to vomit in the room.*)
  So I will trust you. (*She turns to go back in, then back to*
  PEDRO.) But may God punish you, if you don't come back!!
  (*She turns. A large retch from* COLUMBUS. PEDRO *stands for a
  moment, then begins to walk down the stairs, while from the room
  we hear the following:*)
BEATRICE: (*To* COLUMBUS) We're leaving. We'll go get your son
  at the monastery, then we're leaving this country.
  (COLUMBUS *groans.*)
  Sit. Let me hold you. Sit. We're leaving here.
  (PEDRO *is gone.*)

SCENE 2

Projection: THE OCEAN SEA, 200 MILES WEST OF THE
CANARY ISLANDS

The sea. Night. The middle of a violent storm.

*In a flash of lightning, the bow of the huge dug-out boat is seen:
perhaps if all of it could be seen it would be up to sixty feet in length.
Its single sail is in tatters.*

*The seamen (Arawak Indians from the Caribbean) try to hang on,
shout (in Arawak) to hold a rope, to watch a falling piece of mast,
etc., though such shouts cannot really be heard in this wind.*

*Heavy rain, wind and high seas beat the ship – seen only in the
intermittent flashes of lighting.*

*There is a bolt of lightning and the sail catches fire; the storm has
reached a fever pitch as a great wave hits the side of the boat, snapping
the mast in half and capsizing the ship. Screams from the men, barely
heard in this storm, as they go to their death.*

SCENE 3

Projection: THE MONASTERY OF LA RÁBIDA, PALOS,
DECEMBER, 1491

3a

*A small guest room. A bed, a few chairs, a door to a hallway. A few
bags in a corner, unpacked. There is the sense that Columbus is only
passing through; the feeling of refugees.*

    COLUMBUS *sits, and is being shaved by* PEDRO. *Standing near
him is* MARTÍN ALONSO PINZÓN, *age fifty, a local ship captain,
merchant and fisherman.* BEATRICE *sits and sews. Lying down
against a wall and reading is* DIEGO COLUMBUS, *eleven years old.*

    PINZÓN *has just handed* COLUMBUS *a piece of wood.*

PINZÓN: It's the top of an oar. We think.

    (COLUMBUS *turns the object over in his hands and nods.*

    BEATRICE *gets up and goes and looks.*)

BEATRICE: It's very interesting. (*She sits back down and continues
sewing.*)

PINZÓN: They found – . There were things all over the rocks,
they said. I don't know what else – bowls, I think. A statue
of some . . . I don't know. I didn't talk to anyone who – . My
brother did. He said that someone said there was one who
was alive.

    (COLUMBUS *looks up at* PINZÓN.)

Been washed . . . Up.

COLUMBUS: Yes?

PINZÓN: But one of the islanders – . A Portuguese I think is what
I was told – he beat its head in.

    (COLUMBUS *goes back to looking at the object.*)

    (*Pointing to the head of the object*) This little figure is really – .
(*Beat.*) I don't know what it means. If it means anything.

COLUMBUS: Some sailor – to pass the time, carved his oar.

BEATRICE: (*To* PINZÓN) You haven't yourself been to the
Canaries?

    (PINZÓN *shakes his head.*)

COLUMBUS: (*Answering for him*) Not yet.

PINZÓN: No.

14

BEATRICE: It's from the Canaries that – .

PINZÓN: Yes, yes, Señor has told me the complete course he's planning.

COLUMBUS: The currents – . Their boat must have been blown south.

(*Hands the oar to* BEATRICE, *who gets up to take it.*)

Beautiful workmanship. Each day I fear even more the people of the Japan Islands reaching across to us before we have the courage to approach them. (*Beat.*) I misspeak. I do not think it is courage that is lacking. What do you think – Pedro? Pedro's agreed to be my private steward on the voyage, haven't you?

PEDRO: (*Continuing to shave him*) I don't like the water. As long as I don't have to swim.

(*Laughter.*)

I mean it, I don't. Water and me – .

(BEATRICE *has handed* PINZÓN *back the oar head.*)

PINZÓN: (*To* COLUMBUS) If you'd like to borrow it for – . You may like to look more closely, take your time to – .

COLUMBUS: That is very kind, isn't it? (*With the oar head, to* BEATRICE.) This figure, or this face – I suppose it's a face – . It is always so hard to draw the monsters. (*To* PINZÓN) For my maps.

BEATRICE: He's always looking for new models. I've run out of all my monster faces.

(*She shows a monster face.* COLUMBUS *smiles.*)

COLUMBUS: And we are still in need of monsters, Señor – unfortunately. At least for the four corners. If a map doesn't try to scare – what good is it? (*Beat.*) So people seem to think. I'll tell you – from a map-maker's point of view – a way to read a map. Count the monsters. Count all the figures. The little ships, the suns, the faces blowing wind – that's a very good one, that takes up a lot of space. And this is the point, isn't it? The more beautiful, the more involved the drawings on a map – the less useful it is. And this is a lesson of life as well – the artistic urge, isn't it, it's often simply the urge to disguise what we don't know.

(*Beat.*)

PINZÓN: You promised to show me – .

(COLUMBUS *suddenly stands, wiping soap off his face*.)

COLUMBUS: Not here. In private. As I told you. (*Beat*.) Another day. (*Turns to* PEDRO.) Thank you, Pedro. (*Suddenly turns back to* PINZÓN.) I will know when to show you the map, Señor Pinzón. Please do not rush things.

PINZÓN: Of course, I didn't wish to – . I shall be happy to wait.

(*An awkward moment;* PINZÓN *is a little embarrassed. He looks at* BEATRICE, *who has her head down, sewing, then at* PEDRO, *who turns away, etc. Then he puts on a smile and tries to make amends*.)

I have – . You asked to borrow some money.

COLUMBUS: If it's – .

PINZÓN: (*Getting out a purse*) I think it was two ducats.

COLUMBUS: (*Almost at the same time*) For the boy – .

PINZÓN: I'm sorry, but two ducats, it just is impossible, Señor. (*Beat*.)

COLUMBUS: I understand, I only asked – .

PINZÓN: I shall only give you ten ducats, and this is not as a loan – .

COLUMBUS: Ten ducats, I can't accept – !

PINZÓN: It is either ten ducats or nothing, Señor Columbus! (*Beat*.)

COLUMBUS: I thank you.

(*The door opens and* FATHER PEREZ *enters*.)

PEREZ: (*To* COLUMBUS) You have a visitor waiting, Señor.

COLUMBUS: We have been aware of this, Father.

PEREZ: He has been waiting in the hall for – .

COLUMBUS: We know.

PINZÓN: (*Forcing the purse into Columbus's hand*) Now take the money, before you change your mind.

COLUMBUS: Perhaps this should go directly to Father – . (*Begins to hand* PEREZ *the purse*.) We have been so well cared for – .

PEREZ: Your expenses here have already been . . . (*Looks at* PINZÓN.) Please, I believe that is for you.

COLUMBUS: (*Feigning amazement*) God must have brought me here.

PINZÓN: And you, sir, to me.

16

(*An awkward moment with this show of emotion.* COLUMBUS
looks at the oar, holds it up to PEREZ.)

COLUMBUS: Have you seen – ?

PEREZ: Yes. (*Beat.*) I understand you have a map.

COLUMBUS: (*Quickly turns to* PINZÓN) No one was supposed to
know. I asked you – .

PINZÓN: (*Yells*) I told you not to say anything, Father!

PEREZ: I didn't mean – .

PINZÓN: He hasn't told anyone else, have you!

PEREZ: (*At nearly the same time*) I haven't told anyone!

COLUMBUS: Then there's no harm done. But please . . . (*Mouths
'No one else.' They nod. Short pause.* PEREZ *turns to* PEDRO,
who is near him.)

PEREZ: I'm a man of science myself. I study the stars. I make
charts. (*Turns to* COLUMBUS.) I find Hebraic letters – even
whole words – among the constellations.

PEDRO: That's interesting.

(COLUMBUS *clears his throat and* BEATRICE *looks up – taking
the signal.*)

BEATRICE: You shouldn't keep your guest waiting.

COLUMBUS: I'm shaved. I'm just about dressed. I have no more
excuses.

(*Laughs at his joke. He looks at* PINZÓN, *who has not taken the
hint to leave.*)

Until – tomorrow then?

PINZÓN: What?

PEREZ: I think we should – .

PINZÓN: Of course, yes. I'm late already.

COLUMBUS: (*Leading them out, holding the oar head*) I shall
attempt this figure. Come back tomorrow and I shall show
you both the sketch.

PINZÓN: (*Leaving*) So quickly?

(PINZÓN *and* PEREZ *are out the door.*)

(*To* PEREZ) The talent, to be able to draw so – .

(COLUMBUS *closes the door, and tries to stifle a laugh.*
BEATRICE *and* PEDRO *both smile.*)

COLUMBUS: To be back in Seville and away from peasants! I live
in purgatory! (*To* BEATRICE.) Thank God, I at least have you.

BEATRICE: What do you think Pulgar – .

COLUMBUS: And what would I do without you?

BEATRICE: Think Pulgar wants? He's – .

COLUMBUS: Come on – one more monster face.

BEATRICE: (*Stepping back*) He's travelled a long way.

(DIEGO *coughs in the corner*.)

COLUMBUS: (*Turns to* DIEGO) Diego, my son. I nearly forgot you were there! He's so quiet. I suppose this is what a monastery does to one. (*Smiles; no one else does*.)

It's a good place, though. We are lucky. (*To* BEATRICE) He's told me he's been happy here.

BEATRICE: Did he? To me he hasn't said – .

COLUMBUS: I can tell how happy he's been.

PEDRO: (*With a pail of used water; to* COLUMBUS) I'll go down with you and throw this out.

(COLUMBUS *has reached down to see what book* DIEGO *has been reading* – The Travels of Marco Polo.)

COLUMBUS: (*To* DIEGO) Read me a little.

BEATRICE: You've already kept – .

COLUMBUS: A little.

DIEGO: (*Reads*) 'So you must know that when you leave the kingdom of Pasei you come to another kingdom called Samatra, on the same Island. And in that kingdom Seignor Marco Polo was detained five months by the weather, which would not allow of his going on. The people here are wild – .'

COLUMBUS: (*Handing* DIEGO *the oar head*) Here, I give this to my son.

BEATRICE: It's not yours to – .

COLUMBUS: Take it, son. And keep it, treasure it. I shall tell Pinzón I lost it.

(*Beat. He goes to the door.*)

(*Back to* DIEGO) Maybe one day, *you* can return it to where it came from.

(COLUMBUS *leaves;* PEDRO, *with pail, follows.*)

3b

A meeting hall. A table; two chairs. PULGAR *sits;* COLUMBUS *has just entered. They look at each other.*

18

PULGAR: You look – well. Better. You've had some rest.

COLUMBUS: I have never felt better in my life. I never expected to see you here.

PULGAR: Didn't they tell you I – ?

COLUMBUS: Yes, I mean – . I was surprised. When I heard.

PULGAR: Pleasantly surprised, I hope.

COLUMBUS: (*Sitting*) I haven't kept you waiting, have I? I was only just now told you – .

PULGAR: No. I just got here myself.

(COLUMBUS *looks at* PULGAR.)

COLUMBUS: Good. (*Reaching for the pitcher on the table.*) This is water? (*He pours himself a cup.*)

PULGAR: It's quite an attractive place to be – . And the journey here, it wasn't nearly so bad. I was thinking – there are places we tell ourselves we will one day visit . . .

COLUMBUS: And this is one of them.

PULGAR: No.

(PULGAR *smiles.* COLUMBUS *smiles.*)

Still . . . I asked after you – . You haven't been the easiest man to find. I hadn't realized the conditions you had been living in. I went to your apartment.

COLUMBUS: Ah. (*Shrugs.*)

PULGAR: You owed rent. I paid it.

COLUMBUS: That was stupid.

PULGAR: Your landlady certainly looked at me as though I was. (*Smiles.*) Should I talk for a little while more or just tell you why I'm here?

(*No response.*)

How's Beatrice? You know we never met. And after – how many months were we – ?

COLUMBUS: Seven.

PULGAR: Seven months together and in all that time . . . Perhaps while I'm . . . (*Pours himself some water.*) Your son was staying here, in Palos. That's what I remembered. Finally, I remembered this, and so here is where Señor Columbus would be. Or if not, then someone would certainly know . . . (*Beat.*) Even I'm not listening to what I'm saying.

19

(COLUMBUS *takes out the purse* PINZÓN *has just given him and with great drama counts out and lines up seven ducats. Short pause*.)

COLUMBUS: Seven. I believe this is everything that I owe you. (*Pushes back his chair and gets up*.) I did not ask you to pay my rent. Take it. In no way do I wish to be in your debt. (*He goes to the door*.)

PULGAR: You owe me nothing.

COLUMBUS: Take it! (*Beat*.) Seven months I wasted with you! Lied to by you!

PULGAR: That's not – .

COLUMBUS: Used by you!!

PULGAR: *I* did not use *you*!!

COLUMBUS: I'm only now recovering.

PULGAR: Again and again I told you I wouldn't finance – .

COLUMBUS: If I had wanted to be someone's secretary – !

PULGAR: Will you listen!!

COLUMBUS: (*Yelling*) Take the money!!! Take it!!!!
(*Short pause*.)

PULGAR: (*Reaching for the money*) If only to get you to stop and –

COLUMBUS: Wait!
(PULGAR *sits back*.)
I won't bore you with how long it took me to save that much. But any effort, no matter how great, is a small price to pay for having this chance to throw it back in your face. (*Beat*.) But . . . Now that I think of it, why should you gain from all you've done to me. Why should you walk out of here seven ducats richer. This does not seem right to me. (*Beat*.) So . . . (*Beat*.) So instead I will give these coins to – the Church. I shall offer them – to the Church. If they accept, if they don't accept, either way, my debt to you is cleared! Agreed?
(PULGAR *smiles and nods*.)
Say it!

PULGAR: Agreed.

COLUMBUS: Why are you smiling?!
(PULGAR *continues to smile and stares at* COLUMBUS – *totally fascinated by this man*.)

PULGAR: I haven't said why I am here. (*He takes out two purses*

20

and puts them on the table.) As we have begun with money. Fifty ducats.

COLUMBUS: Maybe I should get us some wine.
(*He looks around;* PULGAR *continues*.)

PULGAR: You remember, of course, Señor Miguel García.

COLUMBUS: (*With fifty ducats in front of him, he wouldn't remember his own name*) Who?

PULGAR: At dinner – . The man to whom you might have been secretary.

COLUMBUS: I – . Yes. I remember him.

PULGAR: And Soria, his friend. Sit down.
(COLUMBUS *sits;* PULGAR *sips his water*.)
The next morning, after our dinner – I hadn't realized they'd been listening to us – but García brings up – . Asks – . In fact, he shows a great interest in the map we talked about – . Your map and the story of the ancient pilot who gave you – . And so forth. (*Beat*.) At first I think, he's – . It's morning and – . We are just talking. Then he tells me of his own plans. I had known nothing about this. (*Beat*.) He'd been looking to supply a fleet, he'd been thinking about the African coast, of course, but now he'd like to present your map and its story to the court, physically to the Queen and King – he can do that. And apply for a charter.
(*Short pause*.)
Are you listening?
(COLUMBUS *nods*.)
And so I am here to gain the map, the pilot's journal which I know you also claim to have and the story of both which I shall write down in your words. For this . . . (*Shoves over the fifty ducats*.)
(*Pause*.)

COLUMBUS: A charter?
(PULGAR *nods*.)
To venture . . . ?

PULGAR: Across the Ocean Sea. To China. To Japan. To . . .
(*Shrugs*.) Fifty ducats.
(COLUMBUS *stands up*.)

COLUMBUS: (*Half to himself*) To the court? (*Beat*.) But I had come to understand, that you were convinced that such a venture was – .

PULGAR: Madness. Yes. And my opinion has not changed. And I passed on such a belief to my friends.

(*Beat.*)

COLUMBUS: And??

PULGAR: It wasn't for a while, until I realized they might be serious. So – I brought out the reports of the scholars I had approached to review your calculations. (*Beat.*)

I told them how – according to every scholar – you had massively underestimated the size of the Sea. You had extended Asia far beyond its known size, fiddled rather arbitrarily with the accepted distance for a geographic degree, and, when even this wasn't enough to support a journey, the size of the earth, which is all but agreed, you shrank by some thousand or so miles. A voyage which you claim will take no more than twenty to twenty-five days, every single scholar puts at a good four, perhaps even five months! (*Beat.*) I explained this quite carefully. (*Beat.*)

COLUMBUS: And after you explained – ?

PULGAR: I also reminded my friends that you had attempted to present your plan and map once before to the court – I did not tell you, but I had this checked as well, and received a somewhat different account from the one I got from you. One could say that not only were you completely rebuffed, but according to some – actually ridiculed.

COLUMBUS: A map is in effect an artistic expression and as such is a victim of people's tastes. The Queen and King, on the other hand, never saw the map – .

PULGAR: I even told my friends that I also doubted the authenticity of this map, of its story and of the journal – as well as that of the said ancient pilot himself. And suggested – if I did not come right out and say – that one Christopher Columbus was more than capable of fabricating these and any other tales in order to . . . (*Beat.*) And this is where I had to stop. Because in truth I do not know if you really are prepared to set off on such a misguided and doomed adventure as this is or whether the point of all this is but to

22

collect some money and run off. (*Beat.*) I confessed to my
friends that I didn't know.
(*Short pause.*)
I said all this. Again and again and again. And yet – they
were unswayed.
(COLUMBUS *looks at* PULGAR.)
I have known Señor García in particular since I was a boy.
He and my father – . So – I am here, doing what he has
asked. Against my judgement.
COLUMBUS: And with fifty ducats of his money.
PULGAR: (*Nods*) I have seen the map, you will recall. I tell them,
it is not worth anything. But I come. (*Beat.*) I think – you are
a very lucky man.
COLUMBUS: You can take his money back. I don't want it.
(*Pause.*) When my plans – and map – are presented to the
Queen and King, it shall be me who presents them. You've
come for nothing. (*Gets up, goes to the door.*)
PULGAR: (*Without looking up*) Eighty ducats.
(*Beat.*)
COLUMBUS: Don't insult me any more.
(*At the door, he turns back.*)
I have the map with me, of course. I'm available to leave . . .
(*Shrugs.*) Also – and you have not seen this – there is the head
of an oar – carved by natives of Japan. It too was given to me
by the ancient pilot before he died. And it too must never
leave my possession. This I have sworn. (*Beat.*) And I have
also sworn to try to honour his last words to me. He said,
holding out this oar – take it, son, treasure it. Maybe one day
– *you* can return it to where it came from. Good day. (*He
turns to go.*)

3c

*Columbus's small room (same as Scene 3a). Late afternoon, the same
day.*

   COLUMBUS *is at a table – draughting, copying a map. Around him
are* PINZÓN *and* BEATRICE, *who are in conversation, though they
speak in whispers and so what they are speaking about is unheard –
perhaps about their travels or local gossip.*

23

PEDRO *sits and is turning over tarot cards. With him is Columbus's son,* DIEGO. *Standing and watching are* FATHER PEREZ *and* VINCENTE PINZÓN, *thirty-two years old – they too are in whispered conversation, perhaps about the tarot cards.*

All have a glass of wine either in hand or set near them, as they are tasting a new cask that has just been opened.

As the scene begins, in the distance – from the friary's church – a choir of monks begins its chants. One by one, each notices this.

COLUMBUS: (*Listening*) Sh-sh.

> (*All listen to the distant chanting, though continue now with their activities – map-making, turning over cards, drinking, etc. The emotional impression should be of a far greater and more mysterious world just beyond these walls.*
>
> *A light knock on the door. Another one.* BEATRICE *goes to the door, opens it.* PULGAR *is there.*)

PULGAR: Excuse me, I – .

> (BEATRICE *gestures for him to come in, though says nothing.* PULGAR *enters, looks at everyone and nods. They nod back – though without uttering a sound.* PULGAR *immediately feels awkward, not realizing that they are listening to the chanting.*)
>
> Hello. How do you do?

COLUMBUS: (*In a loud whisper*) You haven't met – ? Martín Pinzón – a good friend.

> (PINZÓN *smiles, says nothing.*)
>
> His brother – Vincente.
>
> (VINCENTE *smiles, says nothing.*)

COLUMBUS: Father – .

PULGAR: We've met. The room is comfortable.

> (PEREZ *nods.*)

COLUMBUS: Beatrice . . .

PULGAR: A very great pleasure. I was saying this afternoon that, after all those months in Seville – .

COLUMBUS: Diego, my son.

PULGAR: Your father has often spoken of – .

COLUMBUS: (*Still in a whisper*) Pedro.

PULGAR: Yes. We saw each other earlier. We met outside. While I was . . .

> (*The others are hardly looking at him, as they are listening.*

PULGAR *is even more uncomfortable.*)
I went for a walk. Beautiful countryside. Down to the river.
(*Louder, as if they are deaf or retarded.*) To – the – river.
(*Everyone is back to his or her activity and listening to the
chanting.* PULGAR *goes to* COLUMBUS.)
Could we – ?
COLUMBUS: Señor Pulgar – please – we are listening to the music.
PULGAR: To the – ? The music? (*He laughs.*) You're all listening
to – ! Oh sorry. I'm very – . I thought – . I was beginning to
think it was me you – . Please! Let's listen!
(*The music stops.*)
I think it's over.
(*Smiles. The conversations begin again.*)
PEREZ: (*To* PULGAR) You don't have any wine. We've just
opened a new cask. So we're tasting – . (*Pours a glass.*)
PULGAR: I didn't mean to – . I only came to see Señor – . It won't
take . . . (*Leans over to* COLUMBUS.) Can we speak
somewhere?
(*Without looking up from the map,* COLUMBUS *gestures 'here'.*)
PINZÓN: Vincente has a magnificent voice. Speaking of music.
PEREZ: Don't all the Pinzóns?
PEDRO: (*To* DIEGO, *at the same time*) Who was speaking of music?
PINZÓN: Once we were out in different boats and there was a fog
– to hear him through the fog. Do you remember this?
VINCENTE: No.
PINZÓN: Nothing to see – just that voice.
BEATRICE: I wish I had a voice.
PINZÓN: (*At the same time*) Like an angel!
VINCENTE: I have always believed in the importance of singing.
The first thing I ask a sailor who wants a job is – can you
sing?
BEATRICE: I don't believe that.
VINCENTE: It's important.
PINZÓN: (*Who is peeking over* COLUMBUS's *shoulder*) This is
extraordinary, have you seen this?
PEREZ: (*On his way*) Let me – .
PINZÓN: (*Continuing*) The man has a gift. I love the face on this
fish. It looks a little like you, Father.

PEREZ: (*Getting closer*) It does. I'm flattered.

PULGAR: I don't mean to interrupt – !

(*Beat. They all turn to him.*)

I just wish to tell Señor Columbus that we leave for court in the morning.

PEREZ: For court – ??

(COLUMBUS *holds up his hand, hushing* PEREZ.)

COLUMBUS: 'We'?

(*Beat.*)

PULGAR: I was asked to bring – the map. And if it is only possible by bringing the map-maker, then who am I to forbid it? We leave in the morning. (*Goes to the door.*) I am sure you must be pleased. As I said – you are a very lucky man. (*Turns to go.*)

COLUMBUS: I am busy tomorrow.

(PULGAR *stops.*)

PULGAR: What do you have to – ?

COLUMBUS: Something. I don't recall right now. Something.

(PULGAR *stares at* COLUMBUS.)

PULGAR: The day after then.

(COLUMBUS *shrugs and continues working on the map.*)

When?!

COLUMBUS: (*Looks up*) The day after is fine. I'll let you know the time, Señor.

(PULGAR *hesitates, then leaves.*)

BEATRICE: Why are you – ?

COLUMBUS: To tell the story of the ancient pilot and his map – to the Queen and King of Spain.

(*The others, amazed, look at each other.*)

PINZÓN: (*To* VINCENTE) You've heard about – .

VINCENTE: No, no I haven't. What's – ?

PEREZ: Martín has tried to tell it to me. But he keeps saying: if you only heard Señor Columbus – .

VINCENTE: Why do the Queen and King – ?

COLUMBUS: Martín, you've already heard – .

PINZÓN: Please, please I promise you – . And I've wanted Vincente to hear himself – .

PEREZ: Let me fill up the glasses.

> (*He does. Beat. They all look at* COLUMBUS, *who continues to work on the map.*)

COLUMBUS: I do not want to bore . . .

PINZÓN: That would not be the case.

> (*Beat.*)

PEREZ: We have looked after your boy, señor.

> (COLUMBUS *looks at* PEREZ, *and nods; then he begins the story very quietly, while continuing to work on the map.*)

COLUMBUS: A caravel, sailing from Spain to England – packed with goods. Wind, whatever – hits a storm. A tempest. Like none anyone on the ship had ever experienced before. A mighty and foul force which drove them out into the Ocean Sea, further and further westward. And so they went for many days and many dark nights.

> (*He puts down his drawing tools. All are listening to his every word.*)

Of course many sailors were lost in the storm and much damage was done to the ship. But somehow a few lucky men survived. And when at last this evil oppression released them from its awful grip – (*Beat.*) they found themselves upon the shores of an island which soon they calculated as being – just south of the famed island of Japan. Japan! Rich in spices, gold, jewels. This we know from none other than Marco Polo himself! (*Sips his wine.*)

PINZÓN: How many days did it take to – ?

COLUMBUS: (*Ignoring him*) An island – inhabited by naked people. The sailors lived on roots and barks of trees while they made repairs on their caravel. The return took an even greater toll upon the survivors – again vicious winds clawed at their boat and now all but three – .

> (*The monks begin to chant again.* COLUMBUS *stops.*)

Sh-sh. Why don't I wait . . . ?

PEREZ: No, go ahead.

> (*The others nod.*)

COLUMBUS: (*Continuing now, with the music behind his story*) All but three died on that return; and upon arriving on our shores two, in such terrible condition, died shortly and sadly thereafter. (*Beat.*) The sole survivor – the pilot of the ship – was an older man – or at least that is how he looked to me after his awful experience. Perhaps he was as young as you, Vincente, or as young as me. You could not tell.

(*Beat.*)

As fate would have it be, he knew my brother somehow – from years before – though my brother remembers nothing of this – and, in his search for him, found me instead. One look and my heart bled and I took the pilot in, fed him, clothed him and in so doing he learned of my own interests in the Ocean Sea, in maps, in voyages to distant lands – lands we have read about not only from Marco Polo but also from Mandeville – . (*Beat.*) And so forth. My enthusiasm could not be hidden. Then one day, after weeks in which our relationship had grown past that of a friendship into one of surrogate family, and after days of seeming improvement in his body, he calls me into his room. There, looking no better than the day he arrived at my door, he asked me to sit next to him. From under the bedcovers, he removes what I soon learned was the journal of his amazing journey – which he then hands to me. Next, and even more remarkable, I am given the map clearly charting his voyage both to and from the East. (*Beat.*) He had never mentioned the existence of either before, and now spoke nothing of them except to say: 'They are yours.'

(*Beat. Chanting continues.*)

And then I held my friend like a child in my arms, watched him close his eyes, his breathing cease; and it was in this way, in these arms – that he died. (*Beat.*) Leaving a journal . . . (*He bends down and picks up a wooden book.*) And a map . . . (*Picks up a rolled-up map*) which I must now take to the Queen and King of Spain.

(*Beat.*)

Projection: SANTE FÉ, JANUARY 1492

4a

An anteroom off the central hall; the temporary court at Sante Fé. A makeshift little room, used mostly for storage – a few tables piled on top of each other, the odd chair, etc. The door to the hall is open.

Through the door: fanfares – a sense of excitement and celebration. This will continue throughout the scene, with march music added at times. Sante Fé is into its third or fourth day of celebrating the end of the siege of Granada and the victory over the Moors. Also, through the door, the sense of people hurrying by – much is going on at court.

PULGAR *and* MIGUEL GARCÍA *enter from the hall.*

GARCÍA: (*Entering, shouting over the fanfares*) We are the ones who should be celebrating! Or perhaps we just claim this for us! (*He closes the door and the celebration is muffled.*) It can't go on forever.

PULGAR: That's what they said about the war.

GARCÍA: And it didn't.
(*Pause. They look around; it is clear that they are waiting.*)
I suppose he's meeting . . . Whomever. Whoever wants to meet him. Which should not be a small number after this afternoon. Soria knows what to do. (*Beat.*) Strike while the iron is hot. While they still remember – . The attention spans of these people in court – . (*Shakes his head and laughs.*) He was very good. You have to admit that. I wasn't embarrassed. I thought I might be, but I wasn't. He was genuinely – ? What? What did you think?
(*Beat.*)

PULGAR: You don't want to know.

GARCÍA: The Queen listened throughout his whole story. And the King – he didn't leave. He didn't let it interrupt the conversation he was having, but he didn't get up and go. I'm told that's a very good – .

PULGAR: I'm not interested.
(*Pause.*)

GARCÍA: I loved the oar that was carved with – . What were they –

29

faces? That made an impression, don't you think?

PULGAR: No, I don't. (*Beat.*) I think he was ridiculous. And I can't believe a single person in that court felt anything other than ridicule and scorn and – . And not just for Columbus but for – .

GARCÍA: (*Over him*) But I very much believe we have succeeded!

PULGAR: If you have, it's only because you've asked for no money and yet offered the court a percentage of the profits!!

GARCÍA: This helps, yes.

PULGAR: I don't know why you wanted him here!

GARCÍA: We only asked for the map, as you recall, but – . It's turned out even better like this. And for this we have you to thank.

PULGAR: I don't understand what you are doing.

GARCÍA: The charter will be for a voyage across the Ocean Sea. A new trade route – . Gold, spices, what else? (*Shrugs.*) That's not your question.

PULGAR: I think I'd better go. There's nothing for me here. I have done what you've asked – .

GARCÍA: More than – .

PULGAR: If you'll excuse me – . (*Turns to leave.*)

GARCÍA: Rodrigo.

(PULGAR *stops.*)

I didn't tell you – your friend, Señor Columbus, approached me last night and said – or rather insisted – that he be made captain of this venture.

(PULGAR *turns back.*)

PULGAR: I'm not surprised. I knew he wouldn't know when to stop.

(*Short pause.*)

GARCÍA: So – that is what we have agreed to: Columbus is the captain.

PULGAR: You can't be serious?

GARCÍA: He said – to Soria as well – that he wouldn't appear today, unless – .

PULGAR: He's never captained a boat in his life!!!

GARCÍA: I remember you mentioning that. Soria and I spoke about just that. He didn't mention it himself of course. But

30

we felt what choice did we have? He had us over a barrel, didn't he?

PULGAR: No, he – .

GARCÍA: (*Continuing over him*) So in the papers we filed today with the court – he is listed as our captain.

(PULGAR *doesn't understand, it all seems like a nightmare, nothing makes sense.*

The door opens – from the hall, loud music and more fanfares. COLUMBUS *and* SORIA *enter, both laughing.* SORIA *closes the door – the music again muffled.*)

PULGAR: What's – funny?

SORIA: (*Through his laughter*) A man in there – a counsellor – he reminded Señor Columbus of someone he'd known – .

COLUMBUS: On a ship.

SORIA: On a ship. With a stutter.

COLUMBUS: (*Trying not to laugh*) I didn't tell you this. We asked him to count – (COLUMBUS *looks at* PULGAR *who is just staring at him*) how many sheep there were on the ship. We knew there were six!

(COLUMBUS *and* SORIA *burst out laughing.*)

PULGAR: (*To* GARCÍA, *who is smiling*) I don't understand. But that is not all I don't understand.

SORIA: (*Trying to catch his breath*) Father Talavera is pleased. He nodded to me. At us. That must mean something.

COLUMBUS: (*To* SORIA) Which one was Talavera?

GARCÍA: The priest, next to – .

COLUMBUS: Oh yes, he was very impressed.

SORIA: They gave us more time than I expected.

GARCÍA: That's a good sign of course.

COLUMBUS: (*At the same time, to* PULGAR) You could tell Talavera was impressed.

SORIA: (*Patting* COLUMBUS) That was very clever – giving the Queen the head of the carved oar.

COLUMBUS: Is that what I did? I thought she was only borrowing . . .

GARCÍA: (*Smiling, with his arm around* COLUMBUS's *shoulder*) You did well! Captain, you did us proud! In fact, I don't know what we would have done – .

COLUMBUS: (*Noticing the room*) Why are we in – . (*Gestures 'here'*.)

GARCÍA: They said we should wait.

SORIA: But that doesn't mean you have to – . You've done your
part. The rest is up to us.

COLUMBUS: I don't mind – .

GARCÍA: (*Over this*) I think Pedro's outside. I'm sure he's found
you rooms – .
(*Beginning to lead* COLUMBUS *out*.)

SORIA: (*To* GARCÍA) You've given him money for – ?

COLUMBUS: I can stay – . (*Stops himself, hearing that he is to be
given money*.)

GARCÍA: No, I haven't.

SORIA: Then I'd better. (*Takes out a purse*.)
(*To* COLUMBUS) I'll walk out with you myself, and make
sure Pedro's found somewhere – suitable. And, let's see,
you'll need a good meal – .
(*They are nearly out*.)

GARCÍA: Captain!
(COLUMBUS *turns back*.)
Thank you.
(COLUMBUS *nods and he and* SORIA *exit. The music is louder,
then the door is closed behind them.*
Pause.)

PULGAR: I suppose I'd better – .

GARCÍA: You think we're mad, don't you? Sit down. (*He drags a
chair from the pile*.) I had hoped we could wait, but – . I can
see . . . (*Nods at* PULGAR.) And as we could still use your
help.

PULGAR: I've done all I am going to do for this crazy adventure,
Señor Garcia. I wish you and Señor Soria and 'Captain – '.

GARCÍA: Sit down! (*Beat*.) Please.
(PULGAR *doesn't sit. Another fanfare off*.)
We're not mad. (*Beat*.) Two and a half months ago,
something like that, I learned through a cousin – . He works
here at the court. He was the one – . When I came in, he – .
(*Gestures that they grabbed hands*.)

PULGAR: Yes.

GARCÍA: He visited our house. For a very good reason he visited.

32

He'd learned – and this has since been confirmed – that the court, the Crown – both the King and Queen – have agreed – in principle – upon the total expulsion of . . . Of us. Of Jews. (*Beat.*) From Spain.

PULGAR: I don't understand – .

GARCÍA: Of course, I've converted, but – . You then get into semantics. (*Beat.*) We're Jews. (*Shrugs.*) Once the Moorish wars were over. That's when – . Listen. They're celebrating. (*Beat.*)

It won't happen today of course. In a year. Six months – the earliest. Probably eight. Ten. Let the dust of this settle first. But let a few Jews – along with everyone else – begin to ask for the money they've loaned – to the court for the war. Then there will be a public reason to expel – our greed. Much will be made of this – a public excuse for doing to us what they wish, perhaps have always wished but couldn't before afford. (*Beat.*)

And so it's been agreed. It will happen. To us. Expulsion. If we refuse – death, with no shortage of volunteers to do the killing. If we submit and go – who is going to pay us anything like the value of what we now own, our property, our businesses – ? If you have to sell . . .

(SORIA *returns; music louder. He closes the door.*)

Forced to sell, we will lose – .

SORIA: At least ninety per cent.

GARCÍA: At least. But – if we were to begin to sell our lands and businesses now . . . (*Beat.*) Would this not seem suspicious? Perhaps that we know something which – .

SORIA: And who knows what this suspicion would justify.

(*Short pause.* GARCÍA *looks at* SORIA, *then continues.*)

GARCÍA: What we have chosen to do – is select an enterprise, some enterprise – an exploration across the Ocean Sea, for instance – gain approval of the Crown by – whatever. Offering a healthy percentage, as you have suggested, Rodrigo, is a useful step in this direction, against of course no risk. And – (*Beat*) we are official. We pay everything, they share. They like this. But to raise the money needed – we of course must sell off large amounts of our lands and

33

businesses. How else could we do it? (*Smiles.*) All for a good
cause. And all without suspicion.
(*Pause.* GARCÍA *suddenly sighs.*)
SORIA: Now you understand. A man like your friend, who will
ask few questions – .
GARCÍA: No questions.
SORIA: Whose – enthusiasm is believable. He performed very
well today, he did. I could not have asked for more. (*Turns to*
GARCÍA.)
GARCÍA: Very well.
SORIA: And as long as he sees us spending . . . It is my belief that
he really does wish to attempt this voyage. So much the
better for us.
PULGAR: But then you have no intention of financing – .
GARCÍA: We will pay what we have to, for as long as we have to,
but I can promise that the bulk of our monies will be on their
way to North Africa, long before us. Safe from the bloody
hands of this country and all the countries like it.
(*Short pause.*)
PULGAR: What do you want me to do?
SORIA: Your father was a friend. Sell your property. Get
something for it now. A fair price almost. Save yourself.
(*Turns to* GARCÍA.)
GARCÍA: And keep Columbus – happy. (*Beat.*) Keep him busy.
Do what he wants.
SORIA: And let him keep thinking – .
(*The door suddenly opens; the music is loud again. A* SERVANT *is
at the door, startled to see them here, and they are startled to see
the* SERVANT. *Beat.*)
SERVANT: I didn't know anyone – .
SORIA: (*At the same time*) We were told we could wait – .
GARCÍA: (*At the same time*) Perhaps we should – . I think we've
talked – .
(*Beat.*)
SERVANT: I'm just – getting a chair.
(*Beat.*)
SORIA: Oh.
(*The* SERVANT *chooses a chair, and lifts it. As he does so:*)

SERVANT: I hear there's going to be fireworks later.
>   (*Beat.*)
GARCÍA: I hear that too.
>   (*The* SERVANT *takes the chair out and closes the door; the music is muffled again. The three men sigh.*)

4b

A public room in the inn where Columbus is staying. Later that night. A door and a window. The window looks out into the night – where fireworks are going off in the distance. Through the door, which is closed, a performance of the Enzina play or 'auto', heard in the first scene, is gong on – laughter, music, etc. as in Scene 1a, though much muffled by the closed door. At a table, COLUMBUS, PEDRO *and* JUAN DE LA ENZINA, *the poet and playwright. They sit drinking and eating bits of food.*

COLUMBUS: A very pleasant surprise, meeting you – .
>   (*As laughter bursts out in the other room,* ENZINA *turns toward the door.*)

>   You don't have to be in there – watching or something – ?
ENZINA: I have seen it enough.
COLUMBUS: Ah. (*To* PEDRO) Even the author can't watch – .
ENZINA: (*Offering a plate of food*) I'm only here tonight because an important – someone I am supposed to meet and be friendly with – was said to be coming. (*Beat.*) He's not here. (*Drinks.*) The Cardinal's late. (*Beat.*) Though I should keep checking just in case . . .
>   (COLUMBUS *nods.*)
COLUMBUS: (*Gesture to a bottle of wine*) Would you like some of our – ? Pedro, please pour – .
>   (PEDRO *pours.*)
ENZINA: (*Continuing*) Here's the poem I wrote for him. (*Shows* COLUMBUS.) It's good. He should show up. He paid in advance. (*Beat.*) How is the map-making business?
PEDRO: As of today, Señor Columbus is no – .
COLUMBUS: (*Interrupting*) It is fine. Wars finish. New borders. New maps. I've got work. (*Turns to* PEDRO.) Señor Enzina and I have known each other for – . In Salamanca, that was – .

35

ENZINA: (*At the same time*) How is your brother? He was the real map-maker.

COLUMBUS: (*Overlapping*) In France – he's moved his shop.

ENZINA: (*To* PEDRO) We students lived in his shop!

COLUMBUS: (*Smiling*) The discussions!

ENZINA: (*Smiling*) Only if we brought wine!

(*Laughs.* COLUMBUS *laughs at the memory. Short pause.*)

COLUMBUS: I haven't been back to Salamanca for . . . (*Shrugs.*)

ENZINA: Neither have I.

(*Pause. Fireworks are heard; they listen for a moment.* COLUMBUS *glances at the poem,* ENZINA *takes it away before he can read it.*)

I like this poem. Worth every ducat he paid. He should be very pleased.

COLUMBUS: (*Looking at* ENZINA) I always think of poetry as something – pure. One of the few pure things we have.

ENZINA: You're not a poet.

COLUMBUS: On the page! Its shape. Someone was saying, Juan, at dinner – when was this? And your name came up – they were saying: Juan de la Enzina is wasting – . Talent? His talent – was that it? I don't remember. But I suppose with these – . (*Nods toward the door and the sound of the play.*) You call them something. 'Autos'? They're like nothing we had when I was young. The poets – . I suppose this is where the idea of poetry being pure comes from. From when I was young and 'things' weren't performed in – in the streets. Anyone couldn't just stand there and – .

ENZINA: Pay.

COLUMBUS: (*Ignoring this*) And watch. I should think it all would be quite difficult to – control. In a room like that. In an inn, with people – eating, drinking and . . . (*Beat.*) A man with literary talent – this is so rare, is it not? He should be honoured. His place in the world – among the very highest. Set there – to inspire the rest of us. Such a man, when he appears – the world cannot afford to waste.

(*Looks for a response; gets none.*)

I suppose what I'm saying – as an old friend, which I am – . By the way, this same 'auto', it was being performed while we were in Seville, in the autumn – .

ENZINA: Did you enjoy it?

COLUMBUS: (*Continuing*) So what I am saying, it is not an unconsidered – . I have held this impression for some time.

ENZINA: They asked us to bring it here, because of the celebrations. It's very popular.

COLUMBUS: I am not being clear. (*Beat.*) Let me ask you a question. (*Beat.*) A poem – let's talk about poems. Where does a poem come from?

ENZINA: (*With the poem in his hand*) First someone asks – .

COLUMBUS: I shall tell you. A poem comes from – the soul. Correct? We both know this. This is inarguable. (*Beat.*) The soul. Here is the womb of our creations, our ambitions. Be they artistic – you, or – or be they . . . (*Shrugs.*)

ENZINA: (*To* PEDRO) He hasn't changed.

COLUMBUS: I am trying to help – !

(*Huge laughter from the other room.*)

I defended you at the dinner! I said the man was experimenting, let him try these – . In the end, he shall return – ! I'm not saying I believe what I said, but I defended you!

(ENZINA *nods and smiles.*)

(*To* PEDRO) Didn't I?

PEDRO: I wasn't – .

COLUMBUS: I did! I like you. Look at me – all I wish to argue is that we must protect the womb of our creations. What begins in purity, pure born – we too often corrupt! (*To* PEDRO.) I think about this a lot.

ENZINA: There's also the argument that we begin not pure but rather just clean, and it's nature's way – to dirty us in time.

COLUMBUS: Really? I hadn't heard that. Well – fine! Then our responsibility is to bathe daily – as nature also gave us the bath. And not to revel in filth! (*Beat.*) Is that what I wanted to say? Yes, I think it is. The point being – . And I am older than you, Juan.

ENZINA: And then there's the argument that we begin neither pure, nor clean – but rather just – simple. (*For the first time in the scene he gives* COLUMBUS *his full attention.*) And it is but the natural education from being simple which you wish to call corruption. And life, instead of being a perpetual need for a bath, is rather just like a steadily growing ball of earth rolling down a hill, building, collecting. Becoming magnificent in this way, where contradictions reflect only our inability or lack of talent to see an order, which may appear to us as crossed vines, knots, mazes, but in fact functions as a series of connections, each responding to and affecting the other. And the soul – your womb of creation – is in constant change, being formed by this experience of being in the world and of the world; and though it is born it is not fulfilled until it has passed some time in life and reached a decent age.

(*Pause.* COLUMBUS *has been trying to follow very carefully, but with some difficulty. He nods.*)

COLUMBUS: Very good. Very good. (*Turns to* PEDRO.) This must be what the students are arguing about now.

(*He puts his hand on* ENZINA's *hand.*)

We used to debate like this for hours in our shop. My brother hated it. (*Laughs.*) Excellent. I have missed this. Now let me argue your side and you argue mine.

(*The door opens; a* YOUNG MAN *stands in the doorway – dressed in a costume of the 'auto'. The noise from the play is loud now.*)

YOUNG MAN: (*To* ENZINA) Señor, the Cardinal is here.

ENZINA: (*Getting up*) What an honour. He's come. I have his poem. (*Feels in his pocket.*) How long are you – ?

COLUMBUS: I don't know.

ENZINA: Neither do I. (*Smiles and goes, leaving the door open.*)

COLUMBUS: (*Drinks*) I enjoyed that. It's not often any more you find someone willing to talk philosophy. The mind – arguing like that. It can be a nice escape. (*Beat.*) Did you follow any . . . ? (PEDRO *shakes his head;* COLUMBUS *laughs.*) I meant some of what I said. He was a pretty good poet.

(PULGAR *has entered; he closes the door. The sudden quiet makes* COLUMBUS *and* PEDRO *turn.*)

PULGAR: You room here? It's . . .

COLUMBUS: I'm comfortable. Please . . . (*Gestures for him to join them.*) Pedro . . .

38

(PEDRO *pours wine*.)

PULGAR: (*Sitting*) I could hardly get through out there. I assume you've been watching the fireworks.

COLUMBUS: Beautiful.

PULGAR: I can't stay – . (*Beat*.) García and Soria asked me to . . . To have the pleasure of – . Congratulations – the charter has been granted. (*Short pause*. COLUMBUS *drinks*.) You must be a very happy man.

COLUMBUS: Lucky. To have such a good friend as you, Señor. To have introduced me – . And then brought me here. What we owe you . . .

PULGAR: Is there anything you wish me to do – ? Dates, I'm sure, will now have to be – .

COLUMBUS: Pedro.

(PEDRO *takes out a piece of paper and unfolds it*.)

In all the excitement, I am not sure that I have been absolutely clear about my terms.

PULGAR: (*Smiling*) What terms? It is accepted that you shall captain – .

COLUMBUS: I have prepared for this.

PEDRO: (*Reading*) 'One: that Their Highnesses appoint Don Christopher Columbus the hereditary title of Admiral in and over all islands and mainlands which shall be explored.'

PULGAR: If it doesn't cost the court anything, I'm sure – .

PEDRO: (*Reading*) 'Two: that he should be Viceroy and Governor-General over all the said lands and continents. Three: that he should be entitled to reserve one-tenth of all pearls, precious stones, gold, silver, spices and all other articles and merchandises, in whatever manner found, bought, bartered or gained within his admiralty – the expenses being first deducted. And four: that he should be sole judge in all causes and disputes arising out of traffic between those countries and Spain.'

(*Pause*. PULGAR *takes the paper*.)

PULGAR: One-tenth? You really think – ? (*Stops himself. Smiles and folds the paper*.) Why not? I'll take it to García and Soria. And I shall even go out on a limb and say I would be surprised if these terms were not met.

(COLUMBUS *looks at* PEDRO.)

Thank you for giving the matter the time. We will need to begin raising the funds necessary immediately. García, Soria and I will need to sell – .

(COLUMBUS *looks at* PULGAR.)

That is correct. I have agreed to join this endeavour. We shall be investing our own monies. We shall be selling off property, businesses – . This will take some time.

COLUMBUS: I understand. Just don't take too long.

PULGAR: In the meantime – I shall assist in providing you with whatever you may require.

COLUMBUS: I am honoured by the faith you have in me.

PULGAR: I need to go now and convey the – good news. (*He goes to the door, turns back.*) So you'll be called – the Admiral of – . What?

COLUMBUS: The Ocean Sea.

PULGAR: The Ocean Sea. Good. I just wanted to get it right.
(*He goes, closing the door behind him. Huge laughter from the crowd.*)

COLUMBUS: I thought they'd agree to two, maybe three – .

PEDRO: It shows how much they need you.

COLUMBUS: I suppose. (*Pause. He drinks. Then a big sigh.*)

PEDRO: (*Holds out a glass for a toast*) Sir.

(COLUMBUS *drinks.*)

COLUMBUS: People are always more gullible than you think, Pedro. (*Beat. Whispers.*) If I tell you something, will you swear on pain of death never to tell another soul?

PEDRO: I – .

COLUMBUS: I'm serious. You must swear!

PEDRO: I swear.
(*Short pause.*)

COLUMBUS: The story about the ancient pilot, the story of his map – well, it's not completely – . What's the word? Accurate.

PEDRO: What's not true?

COLUMBUS:, I didn't say it wasn't true, I said it wasn't completely – . Some things are exactly as they did occur. My brother did have a house where I did stay sometimes, and

40

sometimes he was away and friends of his – even seamen – whom I did not know – sometimes would come and ask for him and maybe stay for – . (*Shrugs*.) That is fact. Fact. (*Beat*.) It's the ancient pilot's map that's not quite – that, I sort of – made up.

PEDRO: That you made – ?!

COLUMBUS: The map and – and the ancient pilot himself for that matter. I made him up too. Everything else – just as I described. Fact. (*Bangs the table. Beat. Looks at* PEDRO.) On pain of death!! (*Beat*.) I shouldn't have told you.

PEDRO: No, I swear I – .

COLUMBUS: I finally made a mistake! My first mistake! I shouldn't have told – !

PEDRO: I won't tell anyone!
(*Beat*.)

COLUMBUS: No? Good. (*Half to himself*) The Queen, the King, the court, Soria, García, Pulgar, everyone preparing for a voyage to – . Having been persuaded by . . . I don't enjoy tricking people. I really don't, this is not me. (*Beat*.) But sometimes you just have to sacrifice your personal honour for . . . For the result. I really feel this. (*Beat*.) And sometimes I really feel the opposite. (*Shrugs. Drinks, lost in thought*.) Admiral of the Ocean Sea. Who would have thought . . . ? (*Beat*.) But such is life.
(*Another burst of laughter and music, as well as a quick series of firework explosions*.)

ACT TWO

SCENE I

Projection: PALOS, LATE FEBRUARY OR EARY MARCH, 1492

1a

A hill overlooking the Ocean Sea. Late afternoon; the sound of wind, sea and gulls, and in the distance the bells from La Rábida are being rung. MARTÍN PINZÓN *stands staring out at the sea;* FATHER PEREZ *is near him, with* DIEGO, *Columbus's son.* PINZÓN *hands a letter to* PEREZ, *who hands it to the child.*

PINZÓN: (*Looking out*) I can hardly breathe. My heart is pounding so fast. God has blessed us. It all suddenly looks again like it did to me when I was a boy. To follow that sun – . What young boy hasn't dreamed – ?
(*Turns to* PEREZ.)
We are lucky, Father. God himself has made this happen.

PEREZ: That is why I asked to have the bells rung. (*Beat.*) In thanks to God.

PINZÓN: In thanks – to God!

VOICE: Martín! Martín!
(PINZÓN *doesn't hear. A figure appears on the hill –* VINCENTE.)

VINCENTE: (*Over the noise of the wind and surf*) Martín!
(PINZÓN *turns.*)
Francisco is docking! He'll want to see us all there!
(*As he hurries across, he nearly falls.* PEREZ *looks at* PINZÓN.)

PEREZ: He's coming.

VINCENTE: (*Out of breath*) The launch has already left the – .
(*Stops himself. Looks at* PINZÓN.)
What is it? Is something – ?

PEREZ: Columbus has written to his son. It is very interesting.

PINZÓN: (*With the letter*) I shall show it to you.
Go tell Francisco I'll be there. (*Pointing.*) His hull is low.
He's done well.
(VINCENTE *runs off.*)
(*Staring at the sea*) Admiral of the Ocean Sea.

42

PEREZ: (*To* DIEGO) Your father, Diego!

PINZÓN: Admiral – of that.

1b

A room in the Pinzón home. Through a doorway, a hall where a party is taking place – the crew of Francisco's ship which has just returned from a voyage is celebrating with music and dancing. MARTÍN PINZÓN, VINCENTE *and* FRANCISCO *are in the middle of conversation. Pinzón's wife,* FELIPA, *and* FATHER PEREZ *sit.*

PINZÓN: (*To* PEREZ) My brother does not seem impressed!
(*To* FRANCISCO) Señor Columbus has received a charter from the King and – !

FRANCISCO: I understand that! But I have just got home! I've been sailing for – .

VINCENTE: Martín, let Francisco – !

PINZÓN: What side are you taking?

VINCENTE: I didn't realize there were different – .

PINZÓN: (*To* VINCENTE) You were excited enough when I told you. You agreed that we should write.

VINCENTE: I don't disagree, I still – .

PINZÓN: (*Over this*) I cannot be the only one who decides things for this family!! (*The music continues off.*) We could already be too late.

PEREZ: I would imagine there must be many people interested in such a voyage.

PINZÓN: I am only asking for permission to send a letter. Through Father Perez. He knows where to send – . You have agreed to do this. So I write to him and Columbus agrees that we may join his fleet.

FRANCISCO: Why should he? Why won't he just laugh in our faces? We're not explorers, we're – .

PINZÓN: Experienced captains!!!

FRANCISCO: (*Pointing to* PEREZ) And he says there could be hundreds of offers – !

PEREZ: I don't know for – .

PINZÓN: And because Señor Columbus and I are friends! (*Beat.*) I gave him money. I will remind him of that – should I need to. Father Perez looks after his son.

43

PEREZ: And very well.

PINZÓN: Our father left me six hundred thousand maravedis to
. . . What? He didn't say. We shall be able to lease two ships.
Even three.

FELIPA: Two's enough.

PINZÓN: (*Ignoring her*) Which we agree to outfit and crew. We
present ourselves as captains of these ships and so we join his
fleet. All of this I will put forward in our letter. (*Beat.*) Is this
agreed? (*No response.*) We will be part of a great fleet! Is that
not – ?

PEREZ: So I have heard.

PINZÓN: He has convinced the entire court – the King, the
Queen, their advisors. They've given him a title! (*Beat.*) It is
our good luck for knowing the man, and for having been
decent to him. (*Beat.*) We know about the map he has. He
told us about it. Where is the terrible risk?
   (*A* SAILOR *holding a guitar appears at the door.*)

SAILOR: They asked me to find – .
   (*Turns to* VINCENTE *and holds out the guitar.*)
   They want you to play.
   (VINCENTE *takes the guitar.*)

VINCENTE: (*To his brothers*) You know what I think.

FRANCISCO: No, I don't – .

VINCENTE: Whatever Martín wants . . . (*Beat.*) Whatever you
both decide.
   (*He goes. Pause. As* VINCENTE *begins to play the music off
   becomes faster, a bit wilder.*)

PEREZ: (*To* FRANCISCO) How was the voyage?

FRANCISCO: (*Ignoring him*) I should go and spend time with my
crew. We have asked them here. (*Beat.*) Write the letter,
you're not going to leave me alone until you do.

PINZÓN: I hope it's not just so I'll – .

FRANCISCO: (*Continuing*) But I promise you – he's only going to
laugh in our face. (*He goes.*)

PINZÓN: (*To* PEREZ *and* FELIPA) The Niños have that beautiful
caravel they wanted to lease. I wonder if that's – . Juan Niños
is here. I passed him when we came through. Felipa, you
talk to his wife first. See how desperate he is before we begin

44

bargaining. First I must write. (*Goes to get out paper.*)
(*To* PEREZ, *without looking at him*) Father, pour yourself
some more wine.
FELIPA: (*Holding up her glass*) I'll have some.
PEREZ: Doña Felipa, we haven't heard from you and what you
think about – . All this which is very exciting.
PINZÓN: I'm sure she agrees with me.
FELIPA: I think – my husband should have in writing what
exactly this arrangement is he is making with the Admiral.
PINZÓN: This will – .
FELIPA: What percentage we keep. Where we deduct our costs.
He is always very ready to let things get confused – .
PINZÓN: That's not true!
FELIPA: Time and time again – it ends in confusion. It ends with
anger. You get bitter – .
PINZÓN: I don't know what you're talking – .
FELIPA: I beg you this time, Martín, know what you are asking.
Know what you want and what he wants.
PINZÓN: (*To* PEREZ) A few times – twice at the most – I have
bought land with someone and . . . (*Turns to* FELIPA.) But
this man's an admiral! With a royal charter – !
FELIPA: He gets enthused and excited; he lets that carry him – .
PINZÓN: (*Over this*) Not this time! It won't happen this time!
(*Short pause. The music is very fast now.*)
Here's paper. Let's write.

1C

The hall again, where the party is taking place. VINCENTE *and a
couple of other men with guitars are playing the fast part of 'Morena
me Ilama' – a group of men are dancing – in a very peasant and rough
style. This culminates in the song portion of 'Morena me Ilaman'. As
the song ends:*

45

SCENE 2

Projection: CADIZ

2a

A room in an inn. Early evening. A large table. The middle of a meal – COLUMBUS, DIEGO DE HARANA *and* JUAN SANCHEZ (*cousins of Beatrice*) *and* BEATRICE.

COLUMBUS *is laughing; he reads from Pinzón's letter.*

COLUMBUS: '– my brother and I have leased one ship, we are about to begin negotiations for a second, and –' (*He takes a sip of water to calm himself, then continues.*) '– and we have already begun selecting a first rate crew!' (*Shakes his head, and wipes his eyes.*) What are they thinking? You can imagine the sort of 'first rate' crew . . . (*Turns to* SANCHEZ.) A couple of fishermen, a goatherd . . .

(SANCHEZ *laughs.* COLUMBUS *turns back to the letter.*) 'We await your response' and so on and so on. 'Humbly –' And he signs his name. (*Holds up the letter so all can see.*)

SANCHEZ: Who's Pinzón – ?

COLUMBUS: (*Over this*) I knew him. I think the biggest surprise I've had being – . (*Beat.*) What I hadn't expected at all – was all the begging. The people begging me for – .

BEATRICE: It didn't sound like he was – .

COLUMBUS: Why do you have to defend these people?

BEATRICE: I wasn't defending – .

COLUMBUS: A man you were once quite friendly with, and now they want something from you – and you see how willing they are to debase themselves.

(*To* BEATRICE) You don't agree.

BEATRICE: He gave us money.

COLUMBUS: (*Over this, to the others*) Look at this: 'humbly'! (*Crumples up the letter.*)

BEATRICE: You're not going to answer – .

(PULGAR *has entered some moments before, but only now is he noticed, first by* HARANA, *then by* COLUMBUS.)

COLUMBUS: There you are – .

PULGAR: (*At the same time*) I only just got your message. I'm

46

sorry if I'm – .

HARANA: (*Overlapping*) I remember the day I first met the Admiral – .

SANCHEZ: (*To* PULGAR) The Admiral used to sleep – occasionally – in the back of my apothecary shop. I am already telling people: here is where the Admiral – .

COLUMBUS: *Didn't* sleep! It was uncomfortable!
(*Laughter. It slowly dies down, and they eat.* PULGAR *takes a small piece of bread.*)

HARANA: The Admiral had his boy with him. They needed somewhere to – stay? I introduced him to Beatrice.

COLUMBUS: (*To* PULGAR) Beatrice and Diego – they are cousins.

SANCHEZ: So am I.

COLUMBUS: So are Beatrice and Juan. (*Turns to* PULGAR.) We should get Señor Pulgar something more to eat. We started without waiting – .
(BEATRICE *gets up.*)

PULGAR: I'm really not – . What did you want to see me about – ?

BEATRICE: (*Over this*) Look at what we leave him!

COLUMBUS: (*Over this*) Where's Pedro? He should be serving – .
(BEATRICE *goes.*)
(*To* PULGAR) If I can't control my steward, how shall I control a ship? Don't think that.

PULGAR: I wasn't thinking – .

COLUMBUS: I ask him to take a simple message to one of our ship-owners. I have some questions before we negotiate – .

PULGAR: You should have asked – .

COLUMBUS: Don't worry, you'll get some food in a minute.
(*Short pause. They eat.*)

SANCHEZ: (*With his mouth full, to* PULGAR) You've seen the maps the Admiral's drawn. The skill. When I first saw – .

COLUMBUS: You don't have to keep flattering me, Juan.

SANCHEZ: I wasn't flattering; the truth is not flattery. (*To* PULGAR, *pointing to* COLUMBUS) Humility; now that is rare.

HARANA: And he doesn't drink. (*He drinks.*)

COLUMBUS: (*To* PULGAR) Juan Sanchez is a surgeon. And a good one – I'm told. Isn't he? (*Turns to* HARANA.)

HARANA: He . . .

COLUMBUS: And Diego de Harana . . . A soldier? Would that he fair?

HARANA: Who hasn't been a soldier? (*He laughs.*)

COLUMBUS: I've known them both for years. Beatrice wrote to them. Mentioning the – . My appointment.

SANCHEZ: Which did not surprise us! Though there were some – . (*Turns to* HARANA.) Who was it was saying – about the Admiral, when we told them?

HARANA: (*Over this*) The Admiral has many times told us of his hopes for such a voyage. We were of course very proud.

COLUMBUS: When I was first in Spain – with my son. My wife had died. She was Portuguese. Daughter of a nobleman. (*He eats.*) I haven't remarried.

(BEATRICE *enters with food.*)

I think it was one of my first days in – Córdoba. That's where they're from. How did I get to Córdoba? I'm not sure.

(*Smiles.* HARANA *and* SANCHEZ *smile.*)

(*Nods toward* PULGAR.) Pour him some wine.

SANCHEZ: (*Holds up his cup*) Could I have – ?

COLUMBUS: (*Ignoring him*) And Juan – allowed me – us, my boy and I – to sleep – to try and sleep – in the back of his shop. How much did you charge? I thought it was too much at the time. But what could I do? I'm sure in fact it was very little. (*Beat.*) It was only for a very few days. That's all he allowed us to stay. But I should have been grateful even for that. (*Beat.*) I met their cousin – Beatrice. I had no money, just a – my son. (*To* SANCHEZ) He's at the monastery at La Rábida. I had no choice but to take him there.

SANCHEZ: A nice boy.

COLUMBUS: (*To* HARANA) Why Juan would not let us stay longer in his shop – .

SANCHEZ: (*Interrupting*) I don't remember ever – .

COLUMBUS: (*Over this*) This – at the time – I could not understand! Still, I should have been grateful. I had no more money. I knew no one. What did I expect?!

(*Beat.*)

SANCHEZ: It was never my intention to throw you – .

COLUMBUS: (*To* PULGAR) Speaking of La Rábida. I have read

48

now the letter from the man there. (*Begins to look round for the crumpled letter.*)

PULGAR: Pinzón.

COLUMBUS: A kind man! I enjoyed his company. And he has heard – everyone hears – Diego and Juan heard – about my appointment.

BEATRICE: I suppose one of the priests – .

COLUMBUS: Who hasn't heard? (*Laughs to himself.*) And he has offered – this Pinzón . . . Asked to join – . (*Picks up the letter and smooths it out.*)

PULGAR: I read the letter.

COLUMBUS: Fishermen. From a village. Peasants – who have never even been to court!
(*Suddenly laughs; the others laugh. He calms down.*)
I was moved, I really was. When even the fishermen wish to join us. It made me smile, this letter. A decent man, as I remember – but how we delude ourselves.
(*Pause.* PULGAR *for the first time starts to eat.*)

BEATRICE: He is hungry.

COLUMBUS: What was I – ? We were talking about – ? Beatrice! We met, and Señor Harana, her cousin – I think it was you – you said something quite rude to me when I asked about her.

HARANA: I don't remember – .

COLUMBUS: About my being foreign. I forget the exact slur. Quite insulting. But we forget these things. Especially now – I'm the Admiral. (*Smiles.*)
(*To* HARANA) How is your cake? Let me take a bite.
(*He takes the whole plate from* HARANA *and begins to eat.*)
(*With his mouth full*) Now all of you go away for a while, Señor Pulgar and I have something to discuss.
(*He pushes* HARANA.)

SANCHEZ: I haven't finished – .

COLUMBUS: Out.

BEATRICE: (*Standing, to* HARANA) Take it with you.

COLUMBUS: Out!

PULGAR: We could go – .

COLUMBUS: Stay there! Out!!

49

BEATRICE: (*Pushing* HARANA *and* SANCHEZ) Please, the Admiral
wants you – .

COLUMBUS: You too.

(BEATRICE *hesitates, then she,* HARANA *and* SANCHEZ *leave.*
COLUMBUS *gives a big sigh.*)

They want jobs.

PULGAR: I gathered.

COLUMBUS: And they'll have them. Diego as marshal of the fleet.
Juan as surgeon. (*Beat.*) Beatrice wants this.

PULGAR: You're the Admiral.

(COLUMBUS *stands and moves away.* PULGAR *looks at him.*)

To think – that fishermen – or traders, whatever they are,
and from a village! It is very funny, isn't it?

COLUMBUS: (*Ignoring him, with something else on his mind*) I have
narrowed down my list to fourteen possible ships. I think
you have seen most of them. Eleven are here in Cádiz.
Hopefully your partners will be pleased.

PULGAR: I have no reason to believe otherwise.

(*Beat.*)

COLUMBUS: You choose from them. I don't want to make every
decision.

PULGAR: If that's what you – .

COLUMBUS: (*Interrupting and changing the subject*) An odd thing
yesterday. I was talking with one of the owners. And I
discover from him that there is someone else bidding – .
Then I say: I am representing García and Soria, and the
owner told me to go away. (*Beat.*) Perhaps I did something
wrong? I don't know. I have never purchased a ship
before – .

PULGAR: I'm sure it's nothing you did. Maybe García or Soria –
years ago – something. Involving this owner and – . Who
knows? (*Beat.*) We think you are doing an extraordinary job.

COLUMBUS: (*Not hearing him*) By the way, you know those two
have sold their lands? And at a rather good price, they tell
me.

PULGAR: Good.

COLUMBUS: They do what they say, don't they? But they also –
actually they asked me to bring this up with you – as a friend.

They said – you haven't sold anything yet. Is that true?
(*No response.*)
Now I don't want to have to lecture you, Rodrigo, but I was
asked to bring it up. We are all involved in this together. We
are all counting on each other. I wouldn't want García to
start talking to some other wealthy friend to join – he could
do this. I asked him and he said he could. (*Beat.*) But I
remember that you involved me first. I owe you something
for this, and so this is why I'm telling you – sell your lands!
And put into our venture the money you promised to put in!
(*Short pause.*)

PULGAR: I suppose – it is my nature to put things off. Given half
the chance I'd – .

COLUMBUS: (*Over this*) Whatever. My conscience is clear. But
that is not the reason I – . (*Nods towards the door. He sits back
down.*) I wanted your advice, Rodrigo. (*Beat.*) I have only
been a nobleman for . . . A month? You agree that the title,
Admiral, presupposes a position of nobility?

PULGAR: I suppose it must.

COLUMBUS: Not everyone – . But I do believe that is the
consensus. So – a nobleman. But a nobleman with very little
experience of being – a nobleman. Which is why – . You, in
certain matters, must be far more experienced – .

PULGAR: Me – ?

COLUMBUS: With, your wealth, your place in – .

PULGAR: I'm a Jew.

COLUMBUS: So what? I've seen your estates. (*Beat.*) So – it's
about Beatrice. She's a peasant. (*Beat.*) Now that wouldn't
bother me if – if it were just me. But there's my son. His
mother was a noblewoman. His father is now a nobleman!
And to have Beatrice around him – treating him as she
always has – as a mother might, and not as a servant would
– . She doesn't act like a servant to him at all!

PULGAR: I didn't know Beatrice was your servant.

COLUMBUS: She isn't. She's – . But for my son, she should . . . I
feel this responsibility now. I'm afraid if she – . He needs to
know who he is!! (*Beat.*) So anyway I am thinking of telling
her to leave us. I'm sure she will understand. What has

happened to me – . She has even said how happy she is *for me*! So what I wanted to ask was – what is the practice? Am I to give her money? And if so – how much? I want to do what I am supposed to do. As a man in my position should do.

PULGAR: I don't know. (*Beat.*) I'll ask around.

COLUMBUS: I would appreciate it. Thank you. (*Bangs the table.*) So – now let's get some company back!

(*Claps his hands.* HARANA, SANCHEZ *and* BEATRICE *return.*) We're finished! (*To* PULGAR) That's it. That's what I wanted to ask you. (*To the others*) Come back and join us! There was a story I wanted to tell Juan. Or was it Diego?

(*He laughs.* PULGAR *watches* BEATRICE.)

What did you do out there?

BEATRICE: We were waiting.

HARANA: There weren't any chairs.

SANCHEZ: We stood.

(*They take their seats.*)

COLUMBUS: I remember Juan always chasing us out of the backroom when you had a patient. And my boy and I – we'd have to wait outside. (*Beat. Continuing with his story.*) I was saying: I'd only been made Admiral the week before, I think. We were still in Sante Fé, weren't we?

BEATRICE: We stayed for – .

COLUMBUS: (*Cutting her off*) One of the young – .

PULGAR: (*Interrupting him; to* BEATRICE) For how long? (*Beat.*)

BEATRICE: Two weeks.

(PULGAR *nods;* COLUMBUS *hesitates.*)

COLUMBUS: (*Continuing*) One of the young secretaries of the court – there was something I had to sign. I'm coming out of the door, and this boy, is all he is, he calls: 'Admiral!' (*Beat.*) Just – 'Admiral.' And I kept walking.

SANCHEZ: Because you weren't yet used to being called – ?

COLUMBUS: Let me finish. Kept walking. So he hurries up behind me and taps me on the shoulder. I stop. He says 'Admiral' – again. And I suddenly realize he had been calling me! I just wasn't used to being called 'Admiral' yet! (*Smiles.*) It took – I suppose a couple of weeks.

(*Beat.*)

Columbus's room in the inn. Night. BEATRICE *sits, her dress unbuttoned, her hair down. The door opens and* COLUMBUS *enters carrying a large bucket of water.*

COLUMBUS: I still can't find Pedro – .

BEATRICE: You shouldn't be doing that.

COLUMBUS: I only have the one servant. And if I didn't get it now – .

BEATRICE: You have me.

COLUMBUS: (*Ignoring her*) I was down. I didn't want to have to go back – .

BEATRICE: (*As she helps him set the heavy bucket down*) You're spilling.

COLUMBUS: On my ship I shall have more than one servant!

BEATRICE: The Admiral usually does, doesn't he? In fact, even on land, a man with a title, you usually see – .

COLUMBUS: (*Cutting her off*) That's correct. You do.
(BEATRICE *looks at him: the way he cut her off gives her pause.*)
When a man gains a titled position – . Servants, I think . . .
More than one – they are part of – . (*Stops himself.*) I'm just learning about all that. (*Turns away.*) Your cousins and Pulgar will be right up. I saw them down – . I asked them – .

BEATRICE: We've just spent the whole evening with – .

COLUMBUS: I asked them up! Everything I say, you then have to ask – !

BEATRICE: What?!

COLUMBUS: Put your dress on!

BEATRICE: It is on. (*She begins to button up her dress.*) If you invited them now, why bring the bath – ?

COLUMBUS: For later! I'll use it later!
(*Short pause.*)

BEATRICE: I can wash you. If you want. Later.
(COLUMBUS *does not respond.*) You've been very kind to my cousins. Dinner, asking them – .

COLUMBUS: They're your cousins.

BEATRICE: Thank you.

COLUMBUS: You wanted them hired. I hired them.

BEATRICE: I wanted you only to see – .

COLUMBUS: I hired them.

BEATRICE: I hope not because of me – .

COLUMBUS: I wonder where Pedro could be. I sent him away hours ago. I hope nothing . . .

BEATRICE: Have I done something – ?

COLUMBUS: (*Turning to her*) Put your hair up. They'll be here any minute.

(BEATRICE *begins to put up her hair. They look at each other*.)

BEATRICE: What??? Why are you staring – ?

COLUMBUS: You didn't drink too much, did you? I saw you drinking – .

BEATRICE: No. No, I did not.

COLUMBUS: (*Turns, hearing something out the window*) Sh-sh. (*He looks out the window*.) The fishermen are leaving. The tide must be in. (*Beat*.) Do you realize – that in only a month – . One month! We'll have the ships. The crews. I can't stop myself from staring at the sea. (*Turns back to* BEATRICE.) Do you know where you'll go, while I'm . . .

BEATRICE: I'll be with your son at La Rábida. Where else would I go? We don't have anywhere else where we – .

COLUMBUS: (*Interrupting*) And that would be better than . . . ?

BEATRICE: Where?

COLUMBUS: (*Shrugs*) Your village.

BEATRICE: What village?

COLUMBUS: Where you grew up.

BEATRICE: I have no place there now. I left years – .

COLUMBUS: You must have relatives. Friends. I don't know. What's the name of the village?

BEATRICE: Santa – .

COLUMBUS: Santa Maria! Which reminds me, I've been meaning to tell you – . I have decided to rename one of our ships – and I thought, I'd name it after – your village. I want to do this as a tribute to . . . (*Nods toward* BEATRICE. *Beat*.) For that chapter of my life that has been you. Are you pleased?

(*A knock on the door,* COLUMBUS *hurries and opens it –* SANCHEZ, HARANA *and* PULGAR *are there, holding bottles*.)

Come in! Come in, we're – .

54

HARANA: Seems like we just left each other.

SANCHEZ: We did!

(*Forced laughter.*)

HARANA: We shouldn't stay long.

BEATRICE: It is late.

COLUMBUS: Stay as long as you wish. I don't know about you, but I find it harder and harder to sleep.

SANCHEZ: As it all gets closer – ?

PULGAR: There's a lot to think about, isn't there? I hardly sleep any more.

HARANA: (*Noticing the bucket of water*) Where'd you get the bucket? I was looking – .

COLUMBUS: They have a number of them in the back, by the – .

SANCHEZ: I know where they are. You should have asked me.

(*No one seems to have anything to say. Pause.*)

HARANA: Maybe we're all talked out.

(*A voice in the distance calls out, this is barely heard.*)

COLUMBUS: The fishermen are leaving.

SANCHEZ: It's almost morning then.

BEATRICE: I think it is.

PULGAR: (*To* COLUMBUS) Perhaps I shall – .

HARANA: (*At exactly the same time, to* COLUMBUS) 'Admiral of the Ocean –'

(*They stop, smile.*)

(*To* PULGAR) You first.

PULGAR: (*After a beat; to* COLUMBUS) I was saying perhaps I shall take your advice – and sell my lands soon. I needed to be pushed.

(COLUMBUS *smiles and nods.*)

HARANA: 'Admiral of the Ocean Sea.' Does that – include the beaches?

(*Hard pounding on the door. Everyone stops.* COLUMBUS *goes to the door, opens it.* PEDRO *is there, out of breath and frightened.*)

COLUMBUS: What is – ?

PEDRO: They're gone. Soria and García.

COLUMBUS: Gone where? Back to – ?

PEDRO: They've sailed!!!

PULGAR: What?

PEDRO: On one of the boats that we've been trying to buy. Remember when you mentioned who you were buying it for, and the owner, he – . That other purchaser was García and Soria! They bought it!

COLUMBUS: That doesn't make sense. Why would they bid against themselves?

PEDRO: And they've sailed for North Africa!!
(*To the others*) No one would talk to me. All day, everyone avoided – .

PULGAR: (*Suddenly shouts*) They can't have sailed! It's only been three months!

COLUMBUS: What are you talking about?
(*Everyone has turned to* PULGAR.)

PULGAR: They said it could be a year! Maybe nine months but – . You're wrong! He's wrong! O God help me.

COLUMBUS: What is happening, Pulgar?! Tell me.

PULGAR: (*To himself*) Help me. God help me.

COLUMBUS: (*Screaming at* PULGAR) What is happening?! What do you know?!!!

SCENE 3

Projection: LA RÁBIDA, TWO WEEKS LATER

The balcony of the monastery, overlooking the Rio Jinto and the sea. Morning. COLUMBUS, PINZÓN, VINCENTE PINZÓN, FELIPA, *and* FATHER PEREZ *are in the middle of conversation; they are seated on various chairs and benches.*

PINZÓN: I bought a small farm myself. And I don't need a farm. So I'm looking to sell it. (*Beat.*) But when something is that cheap – . I paid – . Nothing. So you'd be a fool not to. The poor Jew, he had no choice.

PEREZ: No.

PINZÓN: You could see that in his face. He tried to get more out of me, of course – .

PEREZ: (*To the others*) He would, wouldn't he?

PINZÓN: But in the end, he took what I offered. As I said – I

56

don't need a farm. And now I have to go to all the bother of reselling it.

VINCENTE: You're not compaining – ?

PINZÓN: No, no, of course not. Felipa was furious with me – then I told her how much I paid.

(FELIPA *does not react;* PINZÓN *leans over to* COLUMBUS.)

Now she's all for buying ten more such farms!

FELIPA: There aren't many left. They went very fast.

PEREZ: The Church has been offered – . (*Turns to* PINZÓN.) I'd hoped to get your advice. It's a very nice piece of land. Just – . (*Points.*) A vineyard.

FELIPA: Romero's?

PEREZ: His mother was a Jew. He met with one of our priests – .

FELIPA: Quinteros has been after that vineyard for – .

PEREZ: Romero won't sell to him. He said that.

FELIPA: (*To the others*) Quinteros has made an offer – .

COLUMBUS: It's the same in Cádiz.

(*All turn to him.*)

Except with ships.

VINCENTE: They're after our ships here too! Francisco's made – two, three trips across already. They pay by the head.

COLUMBUS: I've had to tell my captains – not to be tempted. If they wish to transport Jews, then they've made a decision and shall no longer be party to this great voyage chartered by the Queen and King of Spain!

(*This has quietened everyone for a moment.*)

PINZÓN: Our two ships – the two ships I promised – they have not done any transporting. And they shall not. (*To* VINCENTE) Will they?

VINCENTE: No! Did any of your captains – ?

COLUMBUS: One did. One chose to – . Tangiers, I think he went to. And what I feared – happened. The boat got damaged. Not badly, but – . (*Shrugs.*) I told the others – do you understand me now?! What if we had counted on having this ship?! Look past your immediate greed and remember what we are trying to – ! (*Stops himself.*) Sometimes it is like speaking into the wind.

(*Beat.*)

VINCENTE: Francisco didn't use either of the two ships we plan to – .

PINZÓN: You can actually see the ships – . (*Stands up and looks out.*) There. It's a little hazy so you can't – . But they're there. Maybe you'd like us to show them to you later – .

VINCENTE: They're just sitting there.

PINZÓN: (*Over this*) Waiting. How long can you stay?

COLUMBUS: My partners think I shouldn't be here now – .

PINZÓN: We are very grateful – .

COLUMBUS: But I've told them – if we are to accept your participation in our venture, then I have the responsibility to at least – discuss plans, meet your crews, visit your ships . . .

VINCENTE: If you wish to come now, we – .

COLUMBUS: This afternoon – is early enough. We arrived quite late.

(*He looks out over the sea.* THE PINZÓNS *don't know whether to stay or go.*)

PINZÓN: Perhaps we should . . . (*Starts to get up.*)

COLUMBUS: I have had arguments with my partners about you. It's important that you kow this. About why we need to add to our fleet – .

PINZÓN: You've told them we ask nothing? We shall supply our own ships. Get our own crews.

VINCENTE: We already have a list of men willing – .

COLUMBUS: I told them this.

FELIPA: And you told them that the Pinzón family – there is no family in Palos better – .

COLUMBUS: My partners are interested in only one thing! But I tell them – my instincts are not those of a businessman, but of a sailor. The wish to have experienced seamen – this is all I am thinking about. And I tell them: you are not like the hundreds of other offers we have received to participate – I actually solicited your involvement.

VINCENTE: (*To* PINZÓN) What does he – ?

COLUMBUS: When one of my partners – . Which one was it? I forget, you'll have to remind me. When he wrote and asked you to consider joining our fleet – he was speaking for me. I hope he made this clear.

PINZÓN: We received no letter from anyone.

VINCENTE: We have had no encouragement – .

COLUMBUS: I don't understand. I instructed someone to write to you and – .

PINZÓN: (*Over this*) Then you are in favour of our being a part of – .

COLUMBUS: I thought it was my idea!!!

(*They break out laughing.*)

Then – totally on your own – ?

PINZÓN: Admiral.

(*They calm down.*)

Ever since your stay here in La Rábida, and the talks we then shared, the voyage which you spoke of and which you are now prepared to take – it has remained with me. Inside me. Like a hot coal. (*Beat.*) Since those evenings, I have harboured dreams of sharing such a voyage with you – with all its glory and honour. I have been – consumed?

(*Turns to* FELIPA.)

Rarely has a day passed without thoughts of such a voyage racing through my mind or certainly through my dreams. And then, when we heard of your commission – I begged Father Perez to have the bells here rung, believing as I do that God had answered my prayers. (*Beat.*) I swear to you, no one has written to us. We have laboured, sir, in the dark. To join your fleet, this has been my ambition, and one so strong it has needed no encouragement.

COLUMBUS: Then I am pleased to learn – .

PINZÓN: We'll bring our ships to Cádiz whenever you say. Now we should let you rest.

COLUMBUS: Why Cádiz? (*He looks out at the sea.*)

VINCENTE: Isn't that where you plan to – ?

COLUMBUS: (*Ignoring him*) From the beginning Cádiz hasn't seemed – . Too – public. Somewhere more like . . . (*Gestures towards Palos.*) How deep is the river?

PINZÓN: You see the caravels.

PEREZ: You're thinking that perhaps Palos – ?

COLUMBUS: I'm thinking out loud.

PEREZ: It would be an honour – .

PINZÓN: Anything we can – .

PEREZ: (*At the same time*) There's room in La Rábida – .

COLUMBUS: And my son is here. I could be with him. But that's a selfish reason.

PEREZ: To want to be with one's son isn't – .

COLUMBUS: And what would my partners say – ?

PINZÓN: Your partners should do what you say!
(*Beat.*)

COLUMBUS: (*Looking at* PINZÓN) There is much to think about. (*He looks back at the sea.* PINZÓN *hesitates, then nods to the others; they all get up to leave, not quite knowing whether to say goodbye to* COLUMBUS *or not. As they go out,* BEATRICE *enters with Columbus's son,* DIEGO. *The others – perhaps too enthusiastically – greet the boy and then are gone. Short pause.*)

BEATRICE: The boy has been waiting to see you.
(COLUMBUS *doesn't hear.* BEATRICE *sits* DIEGO *down in a chair; he has a book.*)

COLUMBUS: (*Looking at the sea*) I like him. He's – more intelligent than I had remembered. I'd remembered – . (*Stops himself.*) It's not as preposterous an idea as I had feared. Even though he is a peasant.

BEATRICE: I'm a peasant.

COLUMBUS: I know. (*Turns to* BEATRICE *and sees* DIEGO.) There you are! Come here, come here!
(DIEGO *hesitates;* COLUMBUS *goes to him.*)
I should have seen you first, but they said – . Didn't they?

DIEGO: What did they say?

COLUMBUS: That you were – doing something. (*He hugs* DIEGO.) Oh Diego, I was beginning to feel so lonely. (*Noticing the book.*) What's this? *The Travels of Marco Polo.*

DIEGO: I brought it so you could read it. I know you like this book.
(COLUMBUS *smiles, opens it and begins to read to himself, chuckling as he reads. Pause.*)

BEATRICE: I think – he brought it for you to read it to him.

COLUMBUS: (*Totally absorbed in his thoughts, he closes the book, and turns to Diego*) Two weeks ago it was going to be a fleet – of noblemen, sons from the most famous families. A secretary for me, a poet, to record – . I had one in mind. (*He smiles, then shrugs, then sighs. Looks out.*) I shall insist that Pinzón supply me with *four* ships. I make this a condition. And that I – and I alone – have final say on the selection of the crew. I've been on ships where – everyone's a relative. For this voyage – I choose! I draw the line there. (*Beat.*) Anything less – it wouldn't be worth it. Anything less – and it wouldn't make sense.

SCENE 4

Projection: 2 AUGUST

4a

A hallway, La Rábida. Late afternoon. Two doors; one to a small room where the captains and owners of each of the three ships, as well as various others (a CAULKER, LUIS DE TORRES – *the translator – etc.) are having final discussions about the preparations for the voyage – which is to begin the next morning. People are in many groups and are speaking at the same time, so nothing can be understood from the hallway and all that can be seen is what passes by the doorway.*

Through the other door is Columbus's room, where PEDRO *and* BEATRICE *are setting up a large table for the final meal. In the hallway is a bench.*

COLUMBUS *has just come out of the small room to greet Beatrice's two cousins,* HARANA *and* SANCHEZ, *who have just arrived and who have been brought down the hallway by* FATHER PEREZ.

HARANA: (*Greeting*) We're not interrupting – .

COLUMBUS: (*Over the noise from the other room*) This has been going on for – .
(*Stops, walks away from the doorway. They follow.*)
Day after day after day. (*Turns back to* PEREZ.) Thank you, Father. I'll see that they're taken care of now.

PEREZ: I wasn't told to expect any more – . So they'll have to stay – .

COLUMBUS: I am sure they understand. You'll join us for the meal, won't you, Father?

61

(*Beat.*)

PEREZ: I haven't been – . I would like to, yes. Thank you. Thank you very much. (*He goes.*)

COLUMBUS: (*Continuing, about the meeting inside*) I've thought fifty times we were finished. Then someone brings up someone else who's – a brother to – someone. Everyone is related to everyone in this town. I smile a lot. And nod. Anyway, I thought you'd never get here.

HARANA: We . . . (*Looks to* SANCHEZ.)

SANCHEZ: We had a chance to make some money. There was some land, it was cheap – .

HARANA: The man's wife's a Jew – .

COLUMBUS: (*He has been listening to the meeting inside, and continues*) It's worse than the court. Not only is everyone related, but then there's the difference between Palos and Moguer – another village, which is – . If you go outside, you can see it, it's – . Father Perez took me aside; he could tell I was not understanding the – . Why this person was acceptable and not that – . He tells me: it'll help to think of it this way, as he thinks of it – of Moguer, he says, as Sparta – to Palos's Athens.

(*He smiles; the others look at each other; then* COLUMBUS *bursts out laughing.*)

I feel a little – light in the head. My mind, it is going very fast. Well – tomorrow! I've got you both approved. They gave me this. (*Hits* HARANA *on the shoulder.*) Marshal. (*To* SANCHEZ) Surgeon. Both with me on the *Santa Maria*.

SANCHEZ: (*To* HARANA) *Santa Maria* – that's the name of our – .

COLUMBUS: We sail in the morning. You know this. On the tide.

SANCHEZ: *Santa Maria* – that'll mean good luck for us.

COLUMBUS: (*Over this, not listening*) It is so good to have you here!

(CRISTOBAL QUINTEROS, *owner of the* Pinta, *comes out of the small room.*)

QUINTEROS: (*Entering*) Señor Columbus – . I'm sorry to interrupt, but there's one more – .

HARANA: Admiral.

QUINTEROS: What?

HARANA: (*Yells*) He's called 'Admiral'!!!

(*Beat.*)

QUINTEROS: (*Taken aback*) Yes. Of course he is.

COLUMBUS: (*Introducing*) Diego de Harana, marshal of the fleet. Señor Quinteros, owner of the *Pinta*.

QUINTEROS: We've been expecting – .

COLUMBUS: Juan Sanchez. Surgeon.

QUINTEROS: The – Admiral – has spoken of you both. We've been waiting. And now – we can stop waiting. (*Turns to* COLUMBUS.) There's a caulker, the young man – .
(*From the small room a burst of laughter and a few cheers.*)

COLUMBUS: (*Over this noise*) Why do we need another caulker? I thought – .

QUINTEROS: We have Viscaino, who is an excellent caulker. He's sailed with me five, six times – .

COLUMBUS: Then we don't need another one. (*To* SANCHEZ *and* HARANA) You see what I'm asked – ?

QUINTEROS: The young man is a relative of the Niños. Juan Niños himself asked if you would talk with – .

COLUMBUS: Why didn't Niños himself come and ask?

QUINTEROS: If you wish him to . . . (*He turns to go back into the meeting.*)

COLUMBUS: (*Stopping him*) I'm sure there's a reason. (*To* HARANA) Sparta – Athens! (*To* QUINTEROS) I'll meet the caulker!

QUINTEROS: And if he meets with your – .

COLUMBUS: How many relatives does Señor Niños have? Never mind.

QUINTEROS: With your approval, Señor Pinzón suggests – and he wishes me to make it clear it is only a suggestion – that he take Viscaino on the *Pinta*, as he had not planned on taking a caulker, but sees the reason now that there is a relative of Señor Niños, and you take the – .

COLUMBUS: Why doesn't Pinzón take Niños' – ?

QUINTEROS: (*Over this*) He believes he has enough Niños on his ship already. (*Beat.*) And I think he's right.

COLUMBUS: Fine. Let's take him. I have decided. I don't even have to meet the – .

QUINTEROS: Señor Niños will insist you meet him. He will want

to be sure you are pleased. And that it is your decision.
(*Beat.*)

COLUMBUS: (*To* SANCHEZ *and* HARANA) This won't take long.

HARANA: (*Wondering where to go*) Should we – ? (*Gestures to 'follow'.*)

COLUMBUS: Why not? I doubt if they'll even notice. Introduce yourselves if they give you the chance – which I'm sure they won't.

(*They all move toward the room.* PEDRO *has come out of the other room and is in the doorway.*)

PEDRO: (*To* HARANA *and* SANCHEZ) It's about time!

HARANA: Pedro!

(SANCHEZ *and* HARANA *go to greet* PEDRO.)

COLUMBUS: (*Over their greetings*) On second thoughts, stay with Pedro – you'll have a better time. No news from the outside world until I'm back!

(COLUMBUS *and* QUINTEROS *go into the small room.*)

PEDRO: (*Greeting*) Welcome to Palos – Rome to Moguer's Venice! (*Smiles, then tries to explain.*) Moguer's a village, just – . It's – .

HARANA: We know.

SANCHEZ: Where's our cousin?

BEATRICE: (*From the other room*) I'm here!

(*They go to her – more greetings and hugs. Suddenly more shouts and laughter from the small room.*)

HARANA: (*Over this*) You seem to have the men. The ships. Six months ago I would have said 'Impossible!'

BEATRICE: There's wine! Come in! Come in! They'll all be in here soon enough.

(*She pulls* SANCHEZ *into the room;* PEDRO *and* HARANA *follows.*)

PEDRO: The people here – they know boats. They know ropes. They know knots. They know wind. (*Stops himself, thinks, continues.*) That's it. The Admiral says that if the journey lasts more than one month, it's not lack of drinking water that'll kill him, it's the conversation.

(*Another burst of laughter from the small room.*)

They're laughing. Someone must have spilled something

down his shirt. (*Beat.*) On purpose.

(*They go into the room. Everyone now comes out of the small room and heads for Columbus's room, where the meal will be. They are all talking among themselves and they include* PINZÓN, VINCENTE *and* FRANCISCO PINZÓN, QUINTEROS, JUAN NIÑOS, LUIS DE TORRES *and many others – quite a crowd.*

A number of conversations go on as they pass through the hall; one of these is the following.)

NIÑOS: They're here? I'd begun to wonder if they'd show up. It's already quite – .

(COLUMBUS *is the last to come out of the room.*)

QUINTEROS: The Admiral knew they would be here.

NIÑOS: Just in case – or if after meeting them we have changed our mind – my cousin would be a very good marshal of the fleet. He knows the men. I think this is a very elemental part of this job, to know the – .

COLUMBUS: (*Over this*) Harana is my marshal. You all agreed – .

NIÑOS: Of course.

FRANCISCO: And he's here.

VINCENTE: And Señor Sanchez, what's he going to be – ?

NIÑOS: A surgeon, wasn't it?

LUIS: We have excellent surgeons in Palos.

(*Most have entered the other room.* COLUMBUS *is cornered by the young* CAULKER. *Also,* LUIS DE TORRES *waits for him at the door.*)

CAULKER: I've wanted to go on such a voyage for – . I just wanted to tell you this. How honoured – . I'm not just a caulker, you know.

COLUMBUS: I didn't – .

CAULKER: I'm also a carpenter. I've worked for a silversmith.

COLUMBUS: Relatives?

CAULKER: Yes, how did you – ?

LUIS: Admiral?

COLUMBUS: (*To* CAULKER, *gesturing for him to leave*) This meal's just for officers – .

CAULKER: Yes, of course, thank you. I – .

LUIS: (*Takes* COLUMBUS's *arm, introducing himself*) Luis de

Torres, sir. We've met, but I'm sure you've met so many – .
I'm the translator.

(*The* CAULKER *has gone down the hall.*)

COLUMBUS: Oh yes. (*Gestures towards the meal.*) I think they're
waiting – .

LUIS: You have been told that I know Latin as well as some
Hebrew. It is the Hebrew, I think, that will be most useful in
Japan.

(*They are gone. Through the doorway, part of the table can be
seen. Conversations continue, food is passed.* PULGAR *enters the
hallway. He is disshevelled from his journey. He hears the voices
and walks slowly toward the door. As he approaches,* PEDRO
*comes out of the room with a mostly empty tray. He stops when he
sees* PULGAR. *Short pause.*)

PEDRO: Señor Pulgar . . . (*Beat.*) I will tell the Admiral.

(*He puts the tray on the bench and goes back into the room.*
PULGAR *sits on the bench, waits, takes his finger and rubs it on the
tray, getting the last bit of the food, then licks it.* HARANA *enters.*)

HARANA: (*After a moment*) This is a surprise. Come to see us off?

(*No response.*)

The Admiral says – . You Jews are supposed to be gone. By
when? It's some time very soon . . .

PULGAR: The date – is by today.

HARANA: By today?

(PULGAR *nods.*)

HARANA: Then you'd better – .

PULGAR: I assumed this is why the Admiral has had to wait all this
time – you leave tomorrow I have heard – from one of the
priests. (*Beat.*) I mean getting the supplies. That must have
been difficult in this – . What with the rush to leave. Every
ship in Cádiz, in Málaga, Almería . . . Packed with Jews. A
real panic. Each day the price goes up. (*Smiles.*)

I have tried to say if we simply refuse, they'd have to postpone
the deadline again, then maybe again, then after a while – who
knows? (*Beat.*) But we panicked. Some boats are so
overcrowded, you see them leaning as they leave. So I
assumed the admiral has had his difficulties getting supplies,
but I'm pleased to see – .

HARANA: I don't know. He sent for us. I just got here too. (*Beat.*)
　　We had some business. There was a – (*Stops himself.*) A
　　farm. Excuse me.
　　(*He goes back into the room. Pause.* HARANA *returns with*
　　SANCHEZ.)
SANCHEZ: Pulgar.
　　(SANCHEZ *nods.* PULGAR *nods back.*)
　　The Admiral says he knows of one boat – today. From Palos.
　　The last one, he says. Maybe you can still – .
PULGAR: It's gone. An hour ago. With the tide.
　　(SANCHEZ *nods. He and* HARANA *go back in.* PEDRO *returns.*)
PEDRO: The Admiral would like to know if you've eaten?
　　(*Beat.*)
PULGAR: No. I haven't.
　　(PEDRO *nods and goes back in. Short pause.* COLUMBUS *comes
　　out.*)
COLUMBUS: I'm sorry you missed the last boat.
PULGAR: Have I?
COLUMBUS: Sanchez just said you – .
　　(*He stops himself, realizes what* PULGAR *is saying.* COLUMBUS
　　looks at PULGAR *with great curiosity.*)
　　Pedro has said you're hungry.
PULGAR: He asked only if I'd eaten.
COLUMBUS: What's the difference? If you're hungry – say so.
PULGAR: I am hungry.
　　(*Beat.*)
COLUMBUS: Then come in – and eat.
　　(COLUMBUS *goes in.* PULGAR *hesitates, then follows. The
　　conversations in the other room continue as they have throughout.*)

4b

*Columbus's room where the meal has taken place – the room seen
through the doorway in Scene 4a. Late evening. The meal is long over.
The last of the officers are leaving:* PINZÓN, VINCENTE,
QUINTEROS, *and* LUIS. SANCHEZ *and* HARANA *are at the table.*
COLUMBUS *sits next to* PULGAR. BEATRICE *is cleaning things away.*
LUIS: (*To* HARANA, *explaining*) Señora Gallego? She was – Father
　　Perez always used to say – she was our Helen of Troy.

QUINTEROS: (*Standing up*) Helen of Moguer. She was from Moguer.

PINZÓN: Though she worked a lot in Palos.

VINCENTE: She did our wash. She was beautiful.

PINZÓN: (*To* VINCENTE) You were maybe – six? She used to bathe Francisco. I used to say – what about me! (*Laughter.*)

(*To* COLUMBUS) Goodnight, and thank you for – .

QUINTEROS: She bathed my brother too. I used to watch. I was fifteen? I remember her hands.

PINZÓN: I remember other parts!

(*Laughter.*)

She was Niños' cousin. (*To* HARANA.) Are you really interested in this?

HARANA: (*He isn't*) I – uh . . .

PINZÓN: (*Continuing*) And he paid her nothing.

QUINTEROS: He's a Niños.

SANCHEZ: Why was she called – Helen of – ? Did the people from Palos steal her away from . . . ?

(*Beat.*)

QUINTEROS: From where?

SANCHEZ: From her home. Moguer.

QUINTEROS: Why would they do that?

VINCENTE: (*To* SANCHEZ) Palos and Moguer – .

PINZÓN: (*At the same time, explaining*) She worked in both villages.

QUINTEROS: (*Same time*) Walked back and forth. (*Beat. To* PINZÓN) What is he talking about – ?

PINZÓN: Goodnight. We must – . (*Takes* QUINTEROS's *arm.*) How did we start talking about – ?

QUINTEROS: I was about to tell you my dream. That I had just this year. There was my wife – in my dream and she's naked. But there between her thighs instead of hair – it is the face of Señora Gallego. When she was young and washing my brother. And her mouth is going like – (*With his hand, gestures that it is talking very fast.*) Goodnight. (*Continues to* PINZÓN.) I told my wife this dream. She said – that it was the last time I got beans for dinner.

68

(PINZÓN *and* QUINTEROS *are gone.* SANCHEZ *and* HARANA *are standing now.*)

HARANA: (*Overlapping with the others' exit*) We should be going as well.

SANCHEZ: Did they tell you where we could sleep?

COLUMBUS: Beatrice will show you. It isn't very – .

(BEATRICE *has set down what she was doing and starts to lead them out.*)

HARANA: (*Gesturing towards the departed guests*) They're not that bad.

SANCHEZ: No, no they're . . . (*Doesn't come up with the word.*) Goodnight.

(*He almost trips over a chair, and exits with* BEATRICE *and* HARANA. *Short pause.*)

COLUMBUS: I should have said – no wine. Tomorrow, we begin with everyone squinting away from the sun and holding their heads.

PULGAR: They seem – (COLUMBUS *looks at him*) happy.

COLUMBUS: It's Quinteros's ship that Pinzón is captain of. Quinteros, he is not terribly pleased about this. They've been – .

PULGAR: They've known each other since – .

COLUMBUS: And he's from Moguer. Quinteros. This means – something. There was something about an aunt of one and the other's uncle – this too seems to have importance. You cannot allow yourself to think about it. The simplest decision becomes – too much. (*Sighs.*)

I should go to bed as well. I'm the admiral tomorrow. (*Smiles.*) I should go and see my son first. He may not be up by the time we sail. And then – to bed. Goodnight. (*He gets up and leaves.*)

(Beat. COLUMBUS *returns.*)

You have nowhere to stay?

(PULGAR *shakes his head.*)

What are you going to do?

(*Chanting off in the near distance.*)

Listen. Father Perez – this is for us. He said he would ask the Brothers. Chants in our sleep, to put prayers in our dreams. I believe he said something like that. A poet, that man.

(*They listen.*)
I think he's the most excited of any of us.
(*He looks at* PULGAR.)
As I already asked – what are you going to do? But then why should I care?

PULGAR: I am – most impressed, Admiral. By – .

COLUMBUS: Three ships. (*Shrugs.*)

PULGAR: Is everything.

COLUMBUS: I think so too.

PULGAR: Do you need one more – sailor?
  (*Long pause.* COLUMBUS *rubs his face, looks away, then back at* PULGAR.)

COLUMBUS: I wondered to myself when you appeared tonight – . At first I said – no, not Pulgar. He – (*Erupts with anger*) had experts! Scholars he called them, to pick apart my plans! To laugh at me!!

PULGAR: Never to – !

COLUMBUS: I had shrunk the world, he told me! I was sick! I was a liar! I faked! You sat there, condescending to speak to me – your disdain you didn't even bother to hide! I listened! I sat there and let myself be humiliated!!!
  (*He stops himself in mid outburst, out of breath. Short pause.*)

PULGAR: Perhaps the – experts – were wrong. I apologize.

COLUMBUS: (*Moves to the door*) I have things to do – .

PULGAR: (*Still sitting, looking down*) I lost my lands, my house. It was too late – what I was offered, I said – to one of my servants, the servant who offered to buy – I said, I'd rather burn it all down!

COLUMBUS: (*Yells*) I don't care!!!!!!
  (COLUMBUS *tries to get a hold of himself.*)

PULGAR: I had nothing. (*Beat.*) I finally thought – I should just kill myself.

COLUMBUS: So instead you come to Columbus! What am I to think about that?!
  (*Pause.*)
But I shall choose – not to think. We are creatures of instinct, are we not? And it is our instincts that we must trust. The rest – what we hear, what we try to think – it's

70

all put there just to – confuse us. Don't you agree?
(*Short pause.*)
You believe now in this voyage? Say 'Yes'.

PULGAR: Yes.

COLUMBUS: And the earth it is – approximately – the size I say it is?

PULGAR: I have no wish to doubt that.

COLUMBUS: Then – I shall hire you – as my secretary. (*He smiles.*)
For – six ducats. (*He takes out a purse, starts to count, stops, puts the purse back.*) I'll pay later.
(COLUMBUS *sits again – he appears very exhausted. Pause.*)
(*Quietly*) You're an educated man, you will add a little class to this whole thing. God knows it needs it. (*Beat.*)
You dream it's going to be – . Queen and King waving!
Banners! Crowds! A big – ! Sons of great landowners serving you! And you get . . . (*Nods toward the door.*)
(*He gets up.*)
You can't sleep here tonight. Father Perez, if he knew a Jew
. . . Sleep on the ship. Pedro's outside. Tell him to send you out in a launch. Now go. (*Moves towards the door.*)

PULGAR: I wish to thank you for – .

COLUMBUS: I said – go! Before I change my mind!
(PULGAR *hesitates then hurries out.* COLUMBUS *listens for a moment to the brothers' chanting, then goes to the door and leaves.*)

4c

The room of Columbus's son, DIEGO. *Night.*
 The chanting continues – it has never stopped since the preceding scene. A candle: the room is full of shadows. COLUMBUS *sits next to his sleeping son.*
 The door opens, more light enters; BEATRICE *enters, also with a candle.*

BEATRICE: Pedro said you wanted to see me.

COLUMBUS: (*Nods towards the boy*) Sh-sh.

BEATRICE: Perhaps we should . . .
(*Gestures that they should go.* COLUMBUS *doesn't look at her.*)
I've been waiting. Then I found Pedro and he said – .

71

(COLUMBUS *still doesn't look at her.*)

They've been chanting for hours.

COLUMBUS: I'm told they shall continue – until we depart. Sit down.

(BEATRICE *sits on a stool.*)

I was carving his features into my brain.

(*He takes her hand.*)

It's late. I must get some sleep. I shall sleep here. But I wanted to see you.

(BEATRICE *nods. The child stirs.*)

(*Quietly*) When the Queen and King appointed me Admiral . . . The weight of this gesture was not hidden from me.

BEATRICE: The responsibility – ?

COLUMBUS: So you understand. (*Beat.*) Being – . Gaining the title of nobleman . . . This title is that of a nobleman.

BEATRICE: I know.

COLUMBUS: So then perhaps what I say will not come as the surprise I've feared. Since receiving the position – because of your own background, your parents, the village you come from and so forth – it makes any relations between us – . Well, wrong.

BEATRICE: What – ?

COLUMBUS: Sh-sh. (*Nods towards the child.*) I shall have to ask you to leave and not be able to explain if you continue – . Please, just listen. I do not want him woken. (*Beat.*) I could never – now – marry – a peasant. That must be clear. And, as a nobleman, to have one even for a mistress – . I feel I violate my honour. I have already – these past six months – felt in violation – .

BEATRICE: You want me to – ?!

COLUMBUS: Enough!

(*He covers her mouth with his hand; then, after a moment, takes it away.*)

I shall not respond to what you wish to say. (*Beat.*) I cannot. (*Beat.*) We must never meet again. (*Beat.*) We must not try to contact each other – ever again. Either through friends or letters or any other means. (*Beat.*) We must forget each other for the remainder of our lives. This is what is right.

(BEATRICE *doesn't know what to do. She wants to scream, but the boy is right there. She is nearly shaking, trying to hold back tears.*)

Beatrice – please. When I return – and this shall be the last time you hear me say your name – never again – when I return, Beatrice – I shall be a different man than the one you've known. With great responsibilities as well as fame. I must accept the trappings that go with these.

(BEATRICE *is weeping. The chanting continues.* COLUMBUS, *desperate as well, looks to* DIEGO *and begins to rush the rest, trying to get through it.*)

COLUMBUS: I have told the boy he cannot see you again. That tomorrow you will be gone. I woke him up and told him. And I sat with him until he fell back asleep.

BEATRICE: Let me talk to him – !

COLUMBUS: No! He too is now a nobleman.

(BEATRICE *weeps;* COLUMBUS *stops. He watches her. He stands and helps her up.*)

Your cousins know nothing of this. I shall need their complete trust on the voyage. Please do not mention any of – . Of what I've said. Before we depart. (*Beat.*) I ask only that. Goodbye.

(*He quickly turns away from her and walks downstage. The room goes dark.* COLUMBUS *is alone in light. He is trying to gather his strength and thoughts. The chanting continues, though now from a greater distance.*

COLUMBUS *begins to address his crews – the audience. It is morning and he stands on the deck of the* Santa Maria *as it waits in Palos harbour; La Rábida is in the distance above.*)

It is a rare opportunity indeed – for any of us to find in life a chance to begin again. To start at a beginning, and breathe the clear air of futures to come, and leave behind the smoke and fog of our pasts. (*Beat.*) And this is where we find ourselves. Our lucky and destined selves – today. This morning. Each man on this voyage has now the ability to shed his skins and become anew, and to be what we wish ourselves to be! (*Beat.*) Those of us not noble-born, shall become noble. Those poor – rich. Those ignorant today shall on return become the wisest of sages in other men's eyes. (*Beat.*) However we got here, whatever our sins or crimes, these shall be washed clean by the first breeze of salt air! Our souls shall take flight! Whomever we leave behind, let our thoughts be directed not back but forward – onward. Wherever we call home, know that it shall be different upon our return – for we shall be different, we shall have new eyes forged out of new sights, our tongues out of new tastes, our ears out of new sounds, our souls – remade by us.

(*Behind him now the giant if not monstrous sail of the* Santa Maria *with its red cross.*)

Let us all be new men! Born today! This minute! And with only one purpose in mind! (*Beat.*) To push forward to triumph! To push forward – to Japan!!!!!

(*Drums begin to pound, cries are heard – they are setting sail.* COLUMBUS *stands alone on the stage – which is now a ship.*)

ACT THREE

SCENE I

Projection: JUST OFF THE CANARY ISLANDS

1a

The Santa Maria; *Columbus's cabin, approximately 10 × 20 feet, just below the poop deck at the far end of the aft. Two little windows and a doorway. A bed, a writing-table, two chairs, a chest.*

COLUMBUS *sits at the writing-table, a book in hand;* SANCHEZ *sits in the other chair;* HARANA *stands behind him.* PEDRO *squats in a corner. There is wine on the table.*

On deck, muffled by the closed door, screaming chickens are being loaded on to the ship.

COLUMBUS *reads from the book – the beginning of the journal he is keeping. He is speaking loudly: over the chickens' screaming.*

COLUMBUS: ' – our Lord, Jesus Christ! Most Christian, most
    high, most excellent and most powerful princes, King and
    Queen of the Spains . . . !' (*Speaks even louder*) 'and of the
    islands of the sea, our Sovereigns.' (*He takes a sip from a cup.*)

PEDRO: (*Nods towards the door*) It's the chickens, they're
    loading . . .
    (COLUMBUS *nods. Then he notices* SANCHEZ *watching him
    drink.*)

COLUMBUS: It's water. But there's . . .
    (*He nods towards the wine.* SANCHEZ *smiles, takes the bottle and
    pours.* HARANA *also wants some;* PEDRO *as well.*)
    'In the present . . .'
    (*He stops, waits for them to pour their wine and settle down.
    Screaming continues off.*)
    'In the present year of 1492 – .'
    (*The door opens,* PULGAR *is there – blood across his shirt. The
    screaming is much louder because the door is open.*)

PULGAR: You wanted to see me? I was in the middle of – .

COLUMBUS: Please, please.
    (*He waves him in.* PULGAR *closes the door – the sounds are
    muffled again.*)

75

PULGAR: One of the chickens they're loading. He got . . . out. I was the closest, so . . .

COLUMBUS: Sit, please. Juan, give him your seat. You haven't missed anything.

(SANCHEZ, *with some hesitation, gets up and gives* PULGAR *his seat.*)

I'm anxious for you to hear this. (*Clears his throat; takes another sip of water.*)

PULGAR: Is that water?

(COLUMBUS *nods.*)

Do you mind if I – ?

(*He wants to wash his hands with a wet cloth.* COLUMBUS *waves his hand – no he doesn't mind.*)

COLUMBUS: (*Continuing*) 'In the present year of 1492 after your Highnesses had put an end to the war with the Moors and had concluded that – .'

(PULGAR, *setting the water down, accidentally knocks it over.*)

PULGAR: I'm sorry! Excuse me!

(*He starts to clean it up.* PEDRO *helps.*)

COLUMBUS: (*Over this*) I'll just keep – .

(*From on deck – over the screaming chickens – now can be heard a screaming pig, and men yelling – the pig is obviously loose.*)

PULGAR: I told them the pig wasn't tied – .

(*A crash against the door. A struggle just outside between pig and man. As this continues:*)

COLUMBUS: I'll skip ahead to – . (*Turns the pages.*) Here. This is – . Listen. (*Over the noise.*) ' – your Highnesses determined to send me, Christopher Columbus, to the said parts of Japan and India, to discover the nature and disposition of them all . . .' (*Looks up and nods – what is coming is interesting*) ' – and the means to be taken for the conversion of them to our holy faith.' (*Beat.*) I thought I'd throw that in.

(*A huge pig scream – the pig is killed. Short pause.*)

PULGAR: I'm listening.

(COLUMBUS *nods and continues.*)

COLUMBUS: 'And ordered that I should not go by land to the east, by which it is the custom to do, but to voyage to the west, by which course, unto the present time, we do not know for certain that anyone hath passed. Your Highnesses, therefore, after having expelled all the Jews from your kingdoms and territories, commanded me to proceed to said parts of Japan and India.' (*He had started to mumble, now turns over a few pages. Under his breath.*) And so forth.

(*Finds something.*)

Here. (*Reads.*) 'I departed, therefore, from the city of Granada for Palos, a seaport, where I supplied three ships, well suited for such service . . .' (*He looks up*) '. . . and with many able seamen . . .' (*He looks up again*) '. . . on Friday, the third of August, half an hour before sunrise, took the route for the Canary Islands to steer my course thence.' (*Beat.*) 'I intend to write during this voyage, very punctually from day to day, all that I may do, and see, and experience. Also, I propose to make a chart in which I will set down the waters and lands of the Ocean Sea; and, further, to compose a book.'

(*Beat. He closes the book.*)

I thought – you'd all be interested in hearing this. That there'll be a – record. (*Beat.*)

That I have recognized and accepted the responsibility to . . . On paper. (*Beat.*)

What looks only like another . . . You go on deck – . You listen – . The chickens. The – . One must keep reminding oneself of the importance – !!!

(*The others look at him.*)

We can't forget. Rodrigo, I'd like to have this translated into Latin. I could do it myself, of course, but there are so many other things . . . (*He turns to* PEDRO.) Pedro, take the early evening measurement, will you? (*He hands him another book and a small chip of wood.*)

PULGAR: Why don't you have the official translator – ?

COLUMBUS: Have you talked to him? Another – relative.

SANCHEZ: Last night he tried to read me something. I don't know what it was. Thank God I can look like I'm listening when I'm not. I just – . It was boring. When people read you things – . They think I'm listening but . . .

(*Short pause. The others look at him.*)

COLUMBUS: (*To* PULGAR) Work at the desk. (*He gets up.*) You can even start now – I don't want to get too far ahead of you.

SANCHEZ: I didn't mean I wasn't listening to – .

(PEDRO *leaves – the door opens, more chicken screaming.*)

COLUMBUS: (*To no one*) We have a charter from the Crown! (*Beat.*) I am the Admiral of the Ocean Sea! (*Beat. Turns to the others.*) Tomorrow, when we wake up – there will be no more land to see out there. No islands known. Nothing! Until – Japan.

(*Looks at* PULGAR.)

How's your place up . . . ? (*Nods towards the deck.*)

PULGAR: I'm comfortable.

COLUMBUS: There's a little room . . . (*Nods towards a corner.*) You could sleep – . Pedro is there. Harana. Sanchez's – . You could have his – .

PULGAR: I'm fine on deck.

COLUMBUS: It hasn't rained – .

PULGAR: I like the rain.

COLUMBUS: I'm scared. What man wouldn't be?

(*Short pause.*)

Sleep here. You've brought books. Bring them. I have books. We can share.

(*Turns to others.*)

Someone was shouting in his sleep last night. On deck. Woke up – quite a few – . Do we know who it was?

HARANA: I told you it was Señor – .

(*Starts to point to* PULGAR.)

COLUMBUS: I've stopped dreaming myself. (*Turns to* SANCHEZ *and* HARANA.) Even about Beatrice.

(*He smiles. They smile.*)

SANCHEZ: A wonderful woman – Beatrice!

HARANA: (*Joking*) As her cousins, if we ever heard the Admiral wasn't treating her right – !

(*They are laughing.*)

COLUMBUS: (*Over their laughter*) There's no chance of that.

(PULGAR *looks at him.*)

No more dreams – for the next twenty-odd days – except the one we're living.

78

(*An explosion is heard in the distance. An eerie silence for a
moment, then many voices on deck shouting.* PEDRO *hurries in.*)

PEDRO: Admiral, you'd better come on deck!!

1b

The deck of the Santa Maria, *immediately following Scene 1a. A few
sailors stand at the railings, looking off – towards the audience. In the
distance, explosions can be heard; there are flashes of light and flame on
the sailors' faces.* COLUMBUS, PULGAR, PEDRO, HARANA *and*
SANCHEZ *break into this group.*

A short pause as they stare out.

COLUMBUS: A volcano. It's near Tenerife. I had heard about . . .
(*Beat.*) Aren't we lucky? We could have sailed past Tenerife a
thousand times without seeing . . .
(*A huge explosion.*)

PULGAR: Like fireworks. A real send-off.

COLUMBUS: I saw the volcano in Sicily, when it erupted. It went on
like that for days. You could read by the light.
(*He turns to the sailors, who are awed by the sight.*)
Beautiful.
(*One sailor nods.* COLUMBUS *turns to* PEDRO.)
Isn't it about time for evening prayers?

PEDRO: It's only – .

COLUMBUS: I think it is.

PEDRO: I'll have the bells rung.
(*He goes off. Short pause. More explosions.*)

COLUMBUS: (*Turns back to the men, and to other men, unseen*) This –
means good luck for us!
(*A bell is being rung.*)
Go, go! That – (*Points to the volcano*) isn't going away. Go! It'll
probably still be erupting on our way back!
(*The men go off to prayers. Off, a man begins to sing the prayers.*)

SINGER: (*Off*) Amen y dio nos de buenas noches, buen viaje, buen
pasaje haga la nao, señor capitán y maestre ya buena
compañía.

COLUMBUS: (*To* PULGAR, *over this*) You saw their faces?
(*The bulk of the crew of the* Santa Maria – *off* – *joins in the singing
of the* Salve Regina.)

79

CREW: (*Singing, off*) 'Salve, Regina Mater Misericordiae,
Vita, Dulcedo, et spes nostra, salve.
Ad Te clamamus exsules Filii Evae,
Ad Te suspiramus Gementes et flentes – '
(*The largest eruption yet. The song is stopped for a moment, then continues.*)
'In hac lacrimarum valle.
Eia ergo, . . .'

1c

The deck of the Pinta. *In the distance – from the deck of the* Santa Maria – *the* Salve Regina *is heard. On the* Pinta, PINZÓN *and* QUINTEROS *stand at the railing, watching the volcano.*
QUINTEROS: Our last sight of land – . And it is blowing up.
(*Beat.*) Some of the men – . It's a frightening thing to watch.
PINZÓN: Sh-sh. Listen. (*Beat. They hear the song from the* Santa Maria.)
QUINTEROS: From the *Santa Maria*. It's early for prayers. It's not even seven – .
PINZÓN: Our men aren't the only ones who have been scared by – that. (*Nods towards the volcano.*) The Admiral's no fool. We should do the same.
(QUINTEROS *goes. After a moment, the bells are rung for prayer.* PINZÓN *continues to watch the volcano as the prayers from the* Santa Maria *continue.*)

1d

The Pinta, *Pinzón's cabin – basically the same as Columbus's on the* Santa Maria. *A short time later. Prayers are now being sung on the deck of the* Pinta, *as well as in the distance on the* Santa Maria – *creating the impression that this spiritual music is now everywhere.*
FRANCISCO: (*Sets down his pen*) I don't understand. Why would the Admiral wish to be so secretive about – .
QUINTEROS: There's an explanation. He must have good reasons – .
(PINZÓN *hurries in.*)
PINZÓN: (*Entering*) What did you find out?
FRANCISCO: I have gone over all the lists of – of what we've been

bringing on board here in the Canaries. We know what we
supplied ourselves in Palos.

PINZÓN: You're confident you have everything from here?

FRANCISCO: I have had men watching – .

PINZÓN: (*To* QUINTEROS) Have you looked over these?

FRANCISCO: (*Over this*) For all three ships. Counting . . . We
know what has come on board. (*Beat.*)
Brother, I have captained my own ships!
(PINZÓN *nods.*)
(*Continuing, taps the papers.*) We also have an idea of what's
been depleted since Palos. At least for the *Pinta* and the *Niña*
– the other – (*He looks up*) I have guessed.
(PINZÓN *has a bottle of wine; he offers to* FRANCISCO.)
I have some. It appears then – given some margin for error.
Whether for instance he plans to ration – .

PINZÓN: He has said nothing to me about rationing.

QUINTEROS: Nor to – .

FRANCISCO: I said – as a for instance. I also haven't included –
whatever: fish we catch. Rainwater. Then without taking
into account – . Given just what has been brought on board –
on only that have I based my estimate.

PINZÓN: I agree, we can't know if there'll be any fish or if it – .

FRANCISCO: We can't.

QUINTEROS: Tell him what you concluded – .

FRANCISCO: We have three ships that have supplies for no more
than – between twenty-six and twenty-nine days at sea.
(*Beat.*) Again – with rationing or with adding what we might
expect to catch – . Perhaps another two, maybe three days.

PINZÓN: (*To* QUINTEROS) How many days have you been told –
by the Admiral – before we reach land? I've heard him say –
twenty-four, another time, twenty-six – .

FRANCISCO: I've heard him say as high as twenty-nine.

PINZÓN: Let's say then – twenty-nine days – at sea. If you are
anticipating a voyage of – twenty-nine days – you do not lay
in supplies for *only* twenty-nine days, do you?

FRANCISCO: Of course you don't, you – .

PINZÓN: You lay in twenty-nine days of supplies, if you are
anticipating a voyage of – what? No more than fifteen,

81

sixteen days at sea? Am I correct? Francisco?

FRANCISCO: I – .

PINZÓN: As a man who has captained his own ships, am I correct?

FRANCISCO: Yes, you're – .

PINZÓN: For anything longer, you would be inadequately supplied.

FRANCISCO: Grossly. So I don't understand why he – .

PINZÓN: Our Admiral – appointed as he was by our King and Queen – appears to have prepared for a voyage of a considerably shorter duration than until now we have been led to believe.

(*Beat*.)

FRANCISCO: Then you think in – fifteen, sixteen days we'll reach – ?

PINZÓN: (*To* QUINTEROS) My brother has captained his own ships – can't you tell?

FRANCISCO: Why didn't he tell us?

PINZÓN: Some reason. I don't know.

QUINTEROS: Perhaps he felt if it got out that land was only fifteen days from – .

PINZÓN: There could be many reasons. But what we do know now is that the Admiral did not trust us enough to tell us. And that – is a shame. We must all now work – to win the Admiral's trust. With a great man such as the Admiral – the burden is with us.

(*Short pause*.)

FRANCISCO: Sixteen days . . .

QUINTEROS: We could be home in a month! Rich!!!

(*A big explosion from the volcano*.)

QUINTEROS: You could feel that hit.

PINZÓN: Like the beast at the gates – trying to frighten us.

QUINTEROS: Listen. Sh-sh. (*Beat*.) They're singing prayers on the *Niña* as well now.

(*The singing is listened to for a moment*.)

Projection: SIXTEEN DAYS LATER

2a

The deck of the Santa Maria. *A* SAILOR *is screaming in pain:*
SANCHEZ *stands over him, attempting to pull out a tooth; others hold*
the screaming SAILOR *down.* COLUMBUS *is there and is making a*
gesture to help; but he clearly doesn't know what to do – he tries to
comfort the SAILOR, *he smiles at the other sailors, etc.* SANCHEZ
strains. HARANA *is at a little distance, watching.*
  As the scene begins:
SAILOR: (*Screams*) Ahhhhhhh!!!!!
SANCHEZ: (*Over this*) It's coming. Hold him. It slipped, hold him
    down, I can't – !
    (*Another scream.*)
    There!!!
    (*He holds up the tooth. The* SAILOR *collapses, breathing heavily,*
    with blood down his chest.)
    (*With the tooth*) Who wants to see?
    (*Sailors start to move away.*)
    He's going to feel better now!
HARANA: (*To* COLUMBUS) The *Pinta*'s back in sight.
    (COLUMBUS *goes over to* HARANA *and looks off. A sailor throws*
    water on the deck to clean up the blood.)
SANCHEZ: (*To the retreating sailors*) Anyone else have a tooth
    problem?
    (*They retreat quicker.*)
HARANA: (*To* COLUMBUS) That's three nights in a row the *Pinta*'s
    raced ahead. What does Pinzón think, we don't notice?
COLUMBUS: Ask him. (*Turns to* SANCHEZ.) Juan! (*Waves*
    SANCHEZ *over to him. To* HARANA) Send a message: we'd like
    to hear what he's been doing. I don't think he could be
    offended by that.
HARANA: And even if he were – .
COLUMBUS: (*Grabs* SANCHEZ *by the shoulder, and speaks louder for*
    the benefit of the sailors) I have a tooth . . . (*Opens his mouth.*)
    Over on this side.

(*The sailors stop retreating and turn.*)

SANCHEZ: (*Pleased*) Admiral, why didn't you say – ?

COLUMBUS: It just started to hurt.

(*Turns to* HARANA, *who has stopped.*)

Go!

(HARANA *hurries off.* COLUMBUS *opens his mouth.*)

Can you see – .

SANCHEZ: (*Sticking his hand in*) This one?

(COLUMBUS *flinches in pain – not from the tooth but from the crude way Sanchez stuck his fingers in.*)

COLUMBUS: Yes. That's the one.

SANCHEZ: Should we go into your – ?

SAILOR: (*Whose tooth was just pulled*) Don't let him touch – !

COLUMBUS: (*With bravura*) No. Do it here! In the fresh air! Let the men see that you are my surgeon as well. That I have complete faith in your skills.

SANCHEZ: (*Reaching for his pliers, to a couple of sailors*) I'll need two or three of you – . Come on!

(*The sailors hesitate, then they go to hold* COLUMBUS.)

COLUMBUS: (*Continuing*) What is good enough for my men, it's – .

SANCHEZ: (*With his fingers in* COLUMBUS's *mouth*) This one?

(COLUMBUS *tries to speak.*)

COLUMBUS: This is the sort of captain I wish to be seen – .

SANCHEZ: Hold still now. It won't – .

(*He pulls.* COLUMBUS *tries to hold back the pain.*)

I didn't get – . Another – .

(*Again* COLUMBUS *fights back the pain, even tries to smile.*)

Once more . . .

COLUMBUS: (*With* SANCHEZ's *fingers in his mouth*) If you can't take the little pains, on a voyage like this, how are you going to take – ?

(SANCHEZ *suddenly groans as he strains to pull out the tooth.* COLUMBUS *screams in great agony.*)

SANCHEZ: (*In a panic, sweating now*) It broke. Hold him, I'll have to dig it out.

(*He searches for a knife as* COLUMBUS *screams and writhes on the deck.*)

84

The Santa Maria, *Columbus's cabin.* PULGAR *is at the table.*
COLUMBUS *has just been helped in by* PEDRO. SANCHEZ *has
followed them in.*

PEDRO: (*To* SANCHEZ) What the hell did you think you were
  doing?!

PULGAR: What's – ?

SANCHEZ: He said his tooth – .

COLUMBUS: (*Points to* SANCHEZ) Get him out. Get out, thank
  you!!

PULGAR: (*To* PEDRO) Here's a cloth.

SANCHEZ: He'll feel better now. The tooth's out, so he'll . . .
  Pretty soon.

COLUMBUS: He cut half of my – .

PEDRO: Hold this against your mouth.

SANCHEZ: I'll just put the tooth on the . . . Here it is. (*He puts a
  piece of tooth on the table. Then digs around in his pocket and
  takes out more pieces which he then sets down. Beat.*) I think
  that's all the pieces. (*Smiles. Goes.*)
  (*Short pause.*)

PULGAR: I didn't know he had a toothache.

COLUMBUS: (*Without looking up*) At least that showed the men . . .
  (*He looks up;* PULGAR *and* PEDRO *are looking at him.*)
  It showed them – . That I could take – as the Admiral – could
  take – . (*Beat.*) It seemed a rare opportunity . . . I didn't
  really have a toothache of course. But that is beside the
  point. One wants the men to know one is worthy of . . .
  (*Beat.*) This makes no sense now, does it?

PULGAR: No.
  (COLUMBUS *squeezes his eyes closed and sighs.* HARANA *enters.*)

HARANA: Launch arriving.

COLUMBUS: (*To* PEDRO) Put some water on this cloth. (*To*
  HARANA) Pinzón?

HARANA: How is the . . .? I heard you – .

COLUMBUS: Is it Pinzón?!

HARANA: From the *Pinta*, but I don't think it's Señor Martín.
  (COLUMBUS *takes the cloth from* PEDRO *and rubs his face.*)

HARANA: (*To* PEDRO) I hadn't known the Admiral had a tooth – .

COLUMBUS: Shut up.

(*He spits up some blood.*)

(*To* PULGAR) Pinzón's not coming.

(*He sighs and wipes his face.*)

(*To* PULGAR) You don't think the men are laughing – ?
Seeing their captain – .

PULGAR: I would have thought – sympathy was more like what
they're feeling.

COLUMBUS: Sympathy?

(PULGAR *nods.*)

Sympathy's a good feeling to have for one's captain. (*As he
rubs.*) My eyes keep watering. I wanted to show them – ! I
wanted them to look up to me!

PULGAR: They do – !

COLUMBUS: I want them to say – to each other as I pass – .

(*A knock at the door. The others look;* COLUMBUS *doesn't react.*)

Or as I stand on deck, at a distance – to say: he's – .

PULGAR: Respect comes with your being captain.

COLUMBUS I wish to earn – .

PULGAR: You have, Admiral, by being captain!

COLUMBUS: Sometimes I feel I have just – tricked everyone.

PULGAR: Who have you tricked? (*To* HARANA) Do you feel
tricked?

HARANA: I – ? No, of course, I – .

PULGAR: (*To* COLUMBUS) Then I don't understand what it is you
want.

(*Another knock.*)

COLUMBUS: Come in!

(QUINTEROS *enters.*)

(*To* PULGAR) What am I worried about? You are right,
Rodrigo.

QUINTEROS: Admiral – .

COLUMBUS: Señor Quinteros, please, sit down. I hadn't
expected –

PULGAR: Do you want me to – leave?

COLUMBUS: Stay, stay. But give him your seat.

(PULGAR *gets up and gives* QUINTEROS *his seat.*)

QUINTEROS: You're surprised? But you requested to see me.

HARANA: We requested to see your captain.

QUINTEROS: I am here to represent him. He sends of course his apologies.

HARANA: I suppose he's napping. Having been up for most of the night.

QUINTEROS: Has he? Why do you say – ?

HARANA: Where has the *Pinta* been heading for each night? (*Beat.*) Each night – for three nights now – as dusk settled, we see – all sails raised and there she goes – into the night.

QUINTEROS: (*To* COLUMBUS) We catch the winds when we can, Admiral.

COLUMBUS: So does the *Santa Maria*, which unfortunately is a little slower, so – . But we have discussed all this and Señor Pinzón knows the need to lay back – we can ill afford to become separated this far from home.

QUINTEROS: I do not believe there is any chance of that happening. (*Short pause.*)

COLUMBUS: (*To* PEDRO) Give him some – wine.

QUINTEROS: I don't need – . (*Stops himself.*) Thank you. (PEDRO *pours him some wine.*)

COLUMBUS: Japan – is another ten days' journey, Señor. At the most. Tell Pinzón to be patient. Any land sighted – . There may be little islands – .

QUINTEROS: We've seen birds. Terns. Such birds cannot fly sixty miles. They come from the north-west – .

COLUMBUS: There may be little islands! (*Beat.*) But Japan is due west. (*Beat.*) With decent wind. If we are not becalmed . . . (*Laughs lightly.*) In approximately eight to ten days. This is the route, and we shall not deviate from it! (*Beat.*)

Does Captain Pinzón understand how it looks to our crews when one of us – one ship – disappears every evening? Don't think they don't notice. Crews notice – . (*Stops himself.*) I wish to keep their confidence and any confusions out of their heads! We sail together. One course. (*Beat.*) What we discover, we discover together. (*Beat.*)

With credit due as to your position – and title. I don't want to start distrusting any colleague. Distrust only breeds distrust and then . . . (*Beat.*) Please pass along to Señor Pinzón, my partner in this voyage, that any more forays into the night would be seen by me with the gravest concern which could precipitate a change in the command of the *Pinta* – a change I would make with great regret.

QUINTEROS: I shall tell – .

COLUMBUS: Also give him my warmest regards. And ask him please to join me one of these evenings – when he's free – for supper? For – company? I have missed him.

(QUINTEROS *nods and turns to the door.*)

And you, Señor Quinteros, perhaps you'd like to stay for supper?

QUINTEROS: I have – two cousins of mine are on your ship. I thought since I was here I'd take the opportunity to – .

COLUMBUS: (*Turning away, over this*) Yes, yes! What was I thinking? Of course you'd want to have supper with your relatives!

(QUINTEROS *hesitates, then nods and leaves.*)

Well? (*Turns to the others.*) How was I? I think I was pretty damn good. If I do say so. For never having captained a ship before, I think I was pretty damn forceful!!

HARANA: (*In shock – it just comes out*) You've never captained a ship be – ?

(*He stops himself.* COLUMBUS *looks at* PULGAR.)

I didn't know that.

(*He tries to smile.*)

You were very . . .

PULGAR: That's a – a secret.

HARANA: Of course.

(*Beat.*)

PULGAR: It bears on nothing.

HARANA: No.

(COLUMBUS *tries to smile, then bangs on the table.*)

COLUMBUS: Eight days. At most. With any kind of wind!

2c

The deck of the Pinta. *Evening. Wind.* QUINTEROS *is climbing up a ladder (out of a trap) on the side of the ship.* PINZÓN *and* FRANCISCO *stand on deck.*

QUINTEROS: (*Arriving*) He forbids you sailing the *Pinta* out of sight.

PINZÓN: This is what he wanted to talk about?

FRANCISCO: (*Over this*) He gave no indication of when we'll reach – ?

PINZÓN: We know when! Any second we could –

QUINTEROS: He says – ten days more. Less with better winds. This is what he says.

FRANCISCO: Does he think we're so stupid we don't – ?

PINZÓN: How did he explain the birds? We just saw another about – . Didn't we?

QUINTEROS: That perhaps there is a little island, but we are still ten days away from – .

PINZÓN: Did you ask him about the weed? It's getting thicker.

QUINTEROS: I forgot to ask – .

PINZÓN: You can smell land! Does he think we can't smell it? (*Beat.*)

QUINTEROS: Obviously, then, he's going to tell us nothing, until we're there.

FRANCISCO: Land is there! And we all know it! (*Beat.*) And we have the faster boat.
(*Beat.*)

PINZÓN: (*To* FRANCISCO) Tell the men to raise all sails.

QUINTEROS: He ordered us – .

FRANCISCO: Raise all sails!!!

(FRANCISCO *hurries off, then from off are heard the cries of orders as the sails are beginning to be raised. The noise becomes louder and louder as first drum rolls are added, then whistles and chants – the sense almost that the ship is being prepared for battle.*)

SCENE 3

Projection: FOUR DAYS LATER, BECALMED

3a

The deck of the Niña. *Brilliant blue sky and bright sun. A sense that the ship is just drifting now in the calm. Men sit around – doing the odd chore with ropes, cleaning pots, etc. – and a man with a flute plays the traditional 'Como la rosa en la güerta', which someone else – a young boy soprano – picks up and begins to sing beautifully. There is a sense of loneliness and loss to this song.*

VINCENTE *and* JUAN NIÑOS *are at the railing, looking out. A sailor enters with Vincente's guitar; he takes it and before the other ends, he begins to strum and sing another traditional song* 'Ah, el novio no quoere diner', *which is a much livelier tune. Soon others join in – a sense that most of the boat is now singing – one or even two sailors begin to dance.*

VINCENTE *walks along the deck as he plays, nodding and smiling to the singing sailors. About halfway through the song, he moves up along the deck and out of sight.*

And the deck, the ship, and the crew now become those of the Santa Maria.

The deck of the Santa Maria. *In the distance, the singing from the* Niña *continues. The men on deck are now silent and look straight up.*

PEDRO *and* SANCHEZ *enter with* COLUMBUS, *actually pulling him out from his cabin.*

COLUMBUS: What do you want me to see? What is it? (*He is laughing.*) What – ?

PEDRO: Now – look up.

(COLUMBUS *looks straight up. What he sees – though this is out of our sight – is a sailor who is high up on the mast and just about to jump. A gasp from those on deck, and now we, the audience, see the sailor fall – upstage. We hear a splash and then see real water splash in the air. Cheers from the sailors.* COLUMBUS *laughs and applauds.*)

COLUMBUS: Who's gone the highest?

SANCHEZ: I think he was the – .

COLUMBUS: (*Loud, with bravado*) Let me try! (*He moves to climb up the ropes.*)

PEDRO: I don't think that would be – .

SANCHEZ: (*At the same time*) He's not serious?

PEDRO: Don't let him! Admiral! Stop him!!

(PEDRO *and* SANCHEZ *grab* COLUMBUS *before he can climb very high.*)

COLUMBUS: What's wrong? I just wanted to – . I order you to let me go. I order you!
(They let go. Beat. He climbs a foot or two, looks up, stops.)
(Half under his breath) Someone grab my leg and stop me!
(PEDRO hesitates.)
Stop me!
(PEDRO touches his leg.)
(To the crew) They won't let me go!
(He laughs, as do the crew. He climbs down.)
Five maravedis for the highest jump!
(A sudden scramble to the rope as men start to hurry up.
COLUMBUS *turns and begins to walk away – while watching the men climb. He passes* PINZÓN *and* FRANCISCO *and so the ship and crew now become those of the* Pinta – .

The deck of the Pinta. *The men are still on the ladders, but instead of hurrying to climb up they are now at work, repairing a sail, bringing it down from the mast, etc. In the distance, both the laughter from the Santa Maria and the singing from the* Niña. PINZÓN *and* FRANCISCO *stand and watch the work.*

FRANCISCO: The sails aren't as damaged as one might have thought after – .
PINZÓN: *(At almost the same time)* We have time now. We're sitting here. God help us.
(QUINTEROS enters.)
QUINTEROS: *(With paper, entering)* A line was sent across.
(FRANCISCO takes the paper.)
PINZÓN: What does he say?
(Beat.)
FRANCISCO: He says – seven days, eight – depending upon when the wind comes back.
PINZÓN: This is not what I asked!
FRANCISCO: It appears he does not wish to answer your – .
PINZÓN: I asked – is he aware that we now no longer have the supplies to get home?
(Short pause. They continue to look out. Song and laughter continue from the other ships.)

Columbus's cabin on the Santa Maria. *Early evening.* SANCHEZ,
HARANA, PULGAR *and* COLUMBUS *are all at the small table having
supper.* PEDRO *serves and, when not serving, sits in a corner and eats
his supper. We are in the middle of the conversation.*

HARANA: (*With his mouth full*) You sit in that stupid – . It makes
   you feel – .

SANCHEZ: Foolish.

HARANA: That's right. And – . Like a child. It's like a swing, isn't
   it? Hanging out there over the water. In this rope swing;
   your trousers off – just your ass hanging there – . You'd
   think, just give everyone a pail!
   (*Shrugs. Eats.*)
   And this happened to me the other day. You're sitting there
   – you're in the middle of doing it and a wave, I swear, it
   breaks right over – so now it's all over my foot. (*Beat.*) It was
   like – . I'm sitting there – doing it, and then whack! While
   it's still coming out.
   (PULGAR *stops eating and looks at* COLUMBUS.)

SANCHEZ: (*Eating*) And the rope itself – the seat. No one cleans
   it. So if it doesn't rain . . .

HARANA: Three, four days without rain – . Unbelievable.
   (*Pause. They eat.*)

COLUMBUS: (*Finally*) We are really running out of things to talk
   about, aren't we?

HARANA: What do you mean?

SANCHEZ: It's really what I dread when I get up in the – .

PULGAR: (*Interrupting*) Have I told you what I dread? (*Beat.*) And
   what I have assumed was never far from any of our minds –
   for too long.
   (*He sips wine. The others wait for him to continue.* HARANA
   breaks the moment and turns to COLUMBUS.)

HARANA: Why don't we just have pails that we could – ?

PULGAR: (*Without looking at anyone – quite dramatically*) I dread
   that last moment – that split second – before judgement. A
   moment we all must know is inevitable, should Japan not be
   – just out there. That moment when – Some of us have died.

The water's gone . . . The food's been gone for days and days.
The sun has blackened our skin and blistered our tongues.

COLUMBUS: Rodrigo – .

PULGAR: Please, I'm sure nothing I can say is any worse than what
they see every night in their dreams, Admiral. (*Beat.*) The
ship, in splinters now, it bobs, like a cork, without direction.
When – and here we go, gentlemen – we begin to feel the
inevitable turn of the boat, it twists, and we on only our
stomachs see that sea rising to just below our eyes, and it
comes rushing at us! It hits! And then there is only water, a
jerk of our muscles only thrusts more of it down our throats,
jams it in and we – . (*Choking sound.*) And – . (*Gasping sound.*)
And, as I have heard, what one feels when one drowns is far
worse than just suffocating, rather more like being hanged –
badly and incompetently. But at least death comes – hurrah!
We Christians at least have that to look forward to as we reach
out and yes – the hand of Jesus Christ our Saviour – .

COLUMBUS: You're a Jew.

PULGAR: I converted.

COLUMBUS: I didn't know – .

PULGAR: When I went back to my estate – . A priest was there – .
He said: were I to convert . . . something. He mumbled the
rest. So thinking there was a way of getting my property back
– or rather keeping it – I – converted. (*Beat.*) What a
wonderful feeling. A cleansing. I felt like a new man –
beginning life again! (*Drinks.*) Then I was told my estate had
already been sold – to the Church, by the way, so that made
me feel better. But not to worry, for though I had lost my
worldly possessions, I had gained the immortality of my soul!
(*Short pause.*)
Anyway – the hand of Jesus Christ himself reaches out for me
and lifts me out of this black hurly-burly of death at sea and
Jesus now walks me up some cloudlike stairs to heaven itself,
where I shall live or whatever forever with God – all three of
them – with the knowledge and bliss that I have been saved.
(*Pause.*)
Actually, now that I listen to myself, I don't see what's to
dread at all, do you? Sounds – . (*Stops himself, shakes his head*

in amazement.) Perhaps the greatest thing that could happen to all of us – Christians – is not to find Japan or any land out there at all.

(*A knock at the door;* HARANA *and* SANCHEZ *are startled.*
PEDRO *gets up and opens the door, a sailor is there, they whisper. Suddenly* COLUMBUS *laughs.*)

COLUMBUS: Señor Pulgar is joking with us!!

(*No one else laughs.*)

PEDRO: Señor Harana.

(HARANA *gets up and heads for the door.*)

PULGAR: (*To* SANCHEZ) Why did I go on and on – you should have stopped me. After all, I'm sure you have the same thoughts every night – while you are trying to fall asleep.

COLUMBUS: Pulgar, stop it!

(SANCHEZ *has really been frightened by* PULGAR.)

SANCHEZ: I usually don't have any trouble falling asleep. I don't think about anything.

PULGAR: Aren't you lucky.

HARANA: (*Calls back*) It's Pinzón himself. He's coming on board.

COLUMBUS: Pinzón? (*To* SANCHEZ) You better . . .

(SANCHEZ *gets up and moves towards the door.*)

SANCHEZ: (*At the door*) I just close my eyes – and I fall asleep. It never occurred to me to think about . . .

(*He and* HARANA *leave.*)

PULGAR: What does Pinzón – ?

COLUMBUS: Why did you scare them? Did you see their faces? They won't sleep for – .

PULGAR: Did you see mine when they were talking about sitting in the rope – ? And the waves hit – . I was trying to eat!

(*A knock on the door; it opens;* PINZÓN *is there.*)

COLUMBUS: Captain Pinzón! Please, please come in! This is a pleasure! We're just finishing . . . . But if you wish – .

PINZÓN: No, no thank you. (*He has entered the cabin.*)

COLUMBUS: You don't mind if I . . . (*He stands and finishes eating his supper. While eating*) I'm sorry about the lack of wind.

PINZÓN: Could I see you alone please?

COLUMBUS: Rodrigo is my secretary, there's nothing I keep . . .

(*Turns to* PULGAR.) Have you finished?

94

PULGAR: I could eat a little more.

(*He eats. So* COLUMBUS *and* PULGAR *are standing over the table and finishing their supper.* PINZÓN *doesn't know what to do. Finally he speaks.*)

PINZÓN: Admiral, you have my promise not to take the *Pinta* on any more evening excursions. Shall we say – she will always remain within your view?

COLUMBUS: (*Eating*) Good. I appreciate that. (*To* PULGAR) We do, don't we?

(PULGAR *nods.*)

PINZÓN: So – now there can be no reason for you distrusting me.

COLUMBUS: Who said I ever – ?

PINZÓN: I have assumed that it was this distrust that – . Let me get quickly to the point. Please, I'm here not out of any lack of confidence, but rather – . You have a number of very experienced seamen on this voyage.

COLUMBUS: I know this, you – .

PINZÓN: It would be a pity – to waste their talents. And so it is for this reason that I come: I think it would be a good idea – good for our ships, our men, good for all of us – if you were now to let me see the map. I myself am quite practised in reading – .

(COLUMBUS *has stopped eating; he looks at* PINZÓN.)
What?

COLUMBUS: (*Turns to* PINZÓN) Which map are you referring to?

PINZÓN: (*Smiles*) The map we have been following. (*Beat.*) The one given to you by the ancient pilot. I heard you tell the story – . The one you showed to the Queen and King. The map that won you the charter!!

COLUMBUS: I wouldn't say it was only the map that won us the – . (*Turns to* PULGAR.) Would you?

PINZÓN: The map, please, Admiral!

COLUMBUS: There were a number of convincing arguments. The Crown was offered a percentage. They were asked to put up nothing.

PULGAR: There was the oar head – .

PINZÓN: Oar head?

PULGAR: The Admiral showed a very interesting carved oar head. In fact, you gave it to the Queen.

PINZÓN: And where did he – find this – ?

PULGAR: The ancient pilot – the one you've just mentioned – the Admiral said he gave it to him.

PINZÓN: When I showed you my oar head, you never mentioned – .

PULGAR: You too had an oar head? What a coincidence.
(*Beat.*)

PINZÓN: Señor Columbus, we have – to the best of my knowledge – perhaps eight or nine days' full provisions left – in other words, we have passed – against my better judgement – the point where we can now turn around . . .
(*Beat.*) We must find land.

COLUMBUS: And we shall. You have my promise.

PINZÓN: I have supported you!!!!
(*Short pause.*)
I confess I'd hoped the *Pinta* would be the first to sight – .
Perhaps that was wrong. But I have addressed that, haven't I?
(*Short pause.*)

COLUMBUS: (*To* PULGAR) He wishes to see the map. What can we do? (*Shrugs.*) Where was it? I put it – . I saw it just the other day – . (*He looks around.*) Rodrigo have you – ?

PINZÓN: How can you not know where the map is?!!

COLUMBUS: I hope – when you do see the map – that you won't be . . . What's the word? You see, it isn't all that – . What's the word? My mind's gone blank. (*Beat.*) Accurate. That's it. In fact, I think it'd be fair to say – don't you agree, Rodrigo? – that it is rather more an impression than . . .
The distances, for example, they are more like – estimates really.
(*He looks for the map.*)
I don't seem to be able to . . .
(*He stops himself; looks at* PULGAR, *then at* PINZÓN.)
Have a drink. Please, have – . Well, I'm going to have a drink.
(*He pours himself some wine.*)

I suppose you'd have to find out sooner or later. Well – . And
we're all grown men here.
(*Drinks*.)
Now I don't want to be coy – but, the way you should think
about it is – is that there really is no map.

PINZÓN: What are you – ?

COLUMBUS: By this I mean – there's a map of course, but it isn't
exactly the ancient pilot's map. He didn't exactly have a
map.

PINZÓN: He told you and you drew what he – ?

COLUMBUS: Something like that. Actually, he didn't really exist.
(*Turns to* PULGAR.) Did you know that?

PINZÓN: I don't understand.

COLUMBUS: He was one of those stories, you know, that you just
tell, to get across . . . You never think anyone is really going
to believe – . And then they do. And – ? (*Shrugs and laughs to
himself*.) Oh well. But the point isn't changed and that is
Japan remains due west – in about six, seven days. Maybe
eight. I just feel that. I mean, it has to be, doesn't it, or what
the hell's going to happen to all of us? (*Smiles*.) So I wouldn't
worry too much. Map or no map, we'll get there. Due west.
(*He puts his arm around* PINZÓN's *shoulder*.)
You'll see. All this 'concern' is for nothing. I wouldn't tell
anyone else about – . People might think – . About me.
About you – for waiting this long to – . To ask. Let me show
you out.
(PINZÓN *pulls away*.)

PINZÓN: Why were you given a royal charter?!!!!
(*Short pause*. COLUMBUS *looks at* PULGAR.)

PULGAR: That's – well it's complicated, isn't it? They liked the
map. They did. They liked the – .

COLUMBUS: Oar.

PULGAR: Oar. But I suppose the real reason was – . Well there
were these Jews. Friends of – mine. They needed to – what?
They heard about – . They had property so – . (*Turns to*
COLUMBUS *for help*.)

COLUMBUS: For Christ's sake we're almost there, Martín! Why
are we having this conversation?! What is the point?!

97

(*Pause.*)

PINZÓN: (*Quietly*) My brothers are on these ships. My friends. Cousins. My wealth. Because of me . . .

COLUMBUS: (*Erupting*) And I raised these ships! For which I am Admiral! Ninety men! Experienced captains! And a royal charter!! To say nothing of titles which pass on to my son!!!! Is not this an accomplishment?!!! Is not this the fact?!!!
(*Short pause.*)
I am sorry if you feel tricked. I have not wished to trick anyone.

PULGAR: He hasn't.

COLUMBUS: Why are you here? It was you who wrote to me begging to be a part of – .

PINZÓN: But you said you'd asked one of your partners to write to us and ask us to join . . .

COLUMBUS: Did I?
(PINZÓN *stands in pure shock.*)
Please, you aren't the first sailor to be thousands of miles from home and think maybe you never should have signed on in the first place. Go back to the *Pinta*. Have some supper. Having watched us eat must have made you hungry.
(*Tries to smile; then serious.*)
We can't go back – you said so yourself. Another week – eight days? I feel it. I know it. I've made calculations.
(*Calls.*) Pedro!
(PEDRO *enters.*)
The captain is leaving.
(PINZÓN *leaves silently with* PEDRO. COLUMBUS *calls after* PEDRO.)
And we're done with supper! (*Beat. To* PULGAR) *You* knew about the ancient pilot – .

PULGAR: I had guessed.

COLUMBUS: (*As if that proves his point and innocence*) There.
(*Beat.*) To put your entire faith in a map you haven't even seen. That doesn't even exist! (*Shakes his head.*) You have to wonder sometimes – what can people be thinking?

SCENE 4

Projection: SIX DAYS LATER

4a

Pinzón's cabin, the Pinta. *Morning.* PINZÓN *at the table;*
FRANCISCO *in front of him.*

FRANCISCO: (*Yelling*) And you're just going to sit there?!

PINZÓN: I do not need to be told by you – .

FRANCISCO: We followed you, we listened to – .

PINZÓN: You each made up your own minds!

FRANCISCO: Convinced by you! Admit that the man is a criminal!

PINZÓN: I blame myself more than him!

FRANCISCO: Because of him, we're going to die.
(*Beat.*)

PINZÓN: I know now that I should have – .

FRANCISCO: Are you listening to me?!

PINZÓN: (*Ignoring him*) There are a hundred things I could have done, that would have – . I now see that.
(*Roll of thunder outside.*)
It's raining. That won't make anyone feel better.
(QUINTEROS *enters.*)

QUINTEROS: (*Entering*) The *Niña* has been sighted.

PINZÓN: After three days you begin to imagine the – . What does she signal?

QUINTEROS: That she found nothing.

PINZÓN: So that is the south-west. Signal back that the north-west has been no luckier. (*Beat.*) We continue due west – as our Admiral has wished.

FRANCISCO: He has no right to be called – .

QUINTEROS: And that is all we do?
(PINZÓN *looks to* QUINTEROS.)

PINZÓN: Get a line to the *Niña*.

QUINTEROS: The sea's a bit rough for – .

PINZÓN: Try!
(QUINTEROS *hurries off.*)

99

The deck of the Niña. *Heavy rain and wind.* JUAN NIÑOS *and sailors are at the railing, leaning over towards a sailor who is barely hanging on to a ladder as he holds a line – that which has been brought over in a launch from the* Pinta.

NIÑOS: Careful!! Hold on! Reach down!!
    (*The sailor almost falls in the storm.*)
    Throw it. Throw it!!
    (*A line is thrown. It is grabbed.*)
    Help him up!! We've got the line!
    (*Wind and rain as* NIÑOS *hurries off.*)

4c

Vincente's cabin; the Niña. *The storm outside.* VINCENTE *and his* STEWARD.

VINCENTE: (*In a rage*) This has never happened to me. Never have I had a pilot deliberately record wrong distances!!!
    (*Stops himself. Tries to control himself.*) Do we know if the same is true for the *Pinta*?
STEWARD: We don't. They've been trying to send us a line.
VINCENTE: (*To himself*) It gets worse, then worse, then worse – !
    (NIÑOS *enters.*)
NIÑOS: (*Entering*) We have a line now with the *Pinta*!
VINCENTE: Good! (*He pours himself some wine.*)

4d

The deck of the Pinta. *The storm continues.* QUINTEROS *and sailors are holding on to the line and pulling at it – as they do so, a bag approaches down the line.*

QUINTEROS: (*Shouting over the storm*) Bring it in! Hold it!!!
    Tighter!! (*He leans over.*) Pull!!!! (*He reaches out and grabs the bag that is tied to the line.*)

4e

Pinzón's cabin, the Pinta. *The storm outside.* PINZÓN *and* FRANCISCO, *who has a letter in his hands – an earlier response from the* Niña.

PINZÓN: (*To himself*) I do not believe what is happening.

FRANCISCO: So it appears – and this occurred weeks ago! – the *Niña*'s pilot, because he wished to compare measurements with the other ships, sent his records to the Admiral. And it appears, according to the *Niña*'s pilot, and Vincente has only now learned this, there was a huge discrepancy between what he had recorded and what the Admiral himself was writing down in *his* log. (*Beat.*) So the Admiral – weeks ago! – gave the order that all future measurements would only be taken by the flagship – by the Admiral!

PINZÓN: I knew nothing about this.

FRANCISCO: It appears that not telling anyone – us! – was part of the Admiral's orders. I just spoke with our pilot; he too received the same orders. Our log is just as useless. He's very scared. He realized our situation long ago, I think.
(*The door opens; the storm is louder.* QUINTEROS *hurries in.*)

QUINTEROS: Your brother's replied again. He says – he'll do whatever you think is best. He's at a loss as to – . (*Stops himself.*)

PINZÓN: I'll speak to our crew. (*Moves towards the door.*)

QUINTEROS: (*To* FRANCISCO) The *Niña*'s just gone on one-third water rations. But I suppose this . . . (*Gestures the storm.*) They've been catching fish.
(*As the three go out.*)

PINZÓN: (*To* QUINTEROS) Not only do we not know where we're going, it seems we don't even know how far we've come.
(*They are out. The storm rages.*)

4f

Columbus's cabin, the Santa Maria.
COLUMBUS, PULGAR *and* SANCHEZ *enter.*

COLUMBUS: (*Entering*) Both ships are back now – our friends are back. And now the lines are going back and forth, back and forth, did you notice? (*He takes off a coat, goes to the table and picks up his log.*)

SANCHEZ: (*With some hesitation*) I was talking to some of the men. They asked to see me. I think they wanted me because they know you and I are – .

COLUMBUS: I know what some of the men think. (*Turns to* SANCHEZ.) We're close! Any moment now. We should keep the door locked.

(PULGAR *goes and locks it.* SANCHEZ *notices this.*)

SANCHEZ: Why should we – ? (*Stops himself.*)

COLUMBUS: (*With the log*) This is what I wanted to read. We just finished it. Sit down, sit. We were getting tired of just ourselves.

(*Smiles at* PULGAR. SANCHEZ *sits.*)

I suggest it shall read even better in Latin. (*Begins to read from the log.*) 'This morning I saw – .' (*Stops himself.*) Let me get us some wine. Where's – ? I'll have Pedro – .

SANCHEZ: I don't need anything to drink. The men are collecting the rainwater.

COLUMBUS: Good. (*Clears his throat and reads.*) 'This morning I saw a frigate bird, which makes terns vomit what they have eaten and then catches this vomit in mid-air. The frigate bird lives on nothing else and, even though it is a sea bird, it does not alight on the water and never is found more than sixty miles from land.'

(*He looks up at* SANCHEZ.)

'A little later I saw many flying fish. They are about a foot long and have two little wings like a bat. These fish sometimes fly above the water at about the height of a lance, rising in the air like a cannon shot. Sometimes they fall on our ships.' (*Beat.*) Once. (*Smiles.*) 'The sea is as smooth as a river, and the breeze is delightful and pleasing. Only the nightingales are lacking.' This was a few days ago, of course.

(COLUMBUS *closes the book and looks at* SANCHEZ.)

That's it. I just thought I'd read you that.

SANCHEZ: These birds you mention can't fly more than sixty miles from land?

(COLUMBUS *nods.*)

Then we can't be more than – !

COLUMBUS: (*Turns to* PULGAR) Which day was that? What's today? It was three days ago.

SANCHEZ: But we've travelled a great deal further than sixty miles in the last three – .

COLUMBUS: A great deal further.

PULGAR: I'll start translating into Latin.

(*He pushes* SANCHEZ, *who stands up, and he sits at the table and begins to work.*)

(*Without looking at* SANCHEZ) We should have been there by now. Perhaps we've passed it. Are passing it right now. Maybe Japan is . . . (*Shrugs.*)

COLUMBUS: Now you know. I wouldn't talk to the crew. I wouldn't – . I'd stay in here. As you said: some of the men – they know – we're friends. We now keep the door locked.

(*Sudden pounding on the door.*)

PEDRO: (*Off*) It's Pedro! Let me in!

(PULGAR *gets up and lets him in.*)

(*Entering*) The young Pinzón – he's in a launch – headed for the *Niña*.

(COLUMBUS *nods and turns away. He goes to a corner and picks up a sword, unsheathes it, looks at it, then sets it on the table.* PULGAR *pushes it out of the way so he can write.*)

4g

Columbus's cabin, the Santa Maria, *and Pinzón's cabin, the* Pinta.

In Columbus's – the continuation of the previous scene. PULGAR *writes;* COLUMBUS *sits on the bed, waiting for battle.* PEDRO *busies himself and* SANCHEZ *waits – perhaps takes that offered cup of wine.*

In Pinzón's – PINZÓN *and* QUINTEROS *enter from the storm.*

QUINTEROS: (*Entering*) The crew seemed to take it – .

PINZÓN: They're scared! As they should be. (*Turns quickly to* QUINTEROS.) I want to know what they talk about now. Now that they know.

QUINTEROS: I found their spirit – . And no one questioned the need to ration.

(*A knock at the door. Pinzón's* STEWARD *enters with another message-bag.*)

STEWARD: From the *Niña*.

(*He hands it to* PINZÓN, *who hesitates then tosses it to* QUINTEROS *to read.*)

QUINTEROS: (*Looking at the message*) Francisco has spoken to

the crew of the *Niña* – you have their support when you wish
to call upon it.

(PINZÓN *nods, then coughs a dry, tired cough – all this is taking
its toll.*)

I will try to see what the men are saying.

(*He and the* STEWARD *go.* PINZÓN, *alone, sits at his table.*)

4h

The deck of the Santa Maria. *The storm continues.* FRANCISCO *is
climbing up the ladder from his launch.* HARANA *and two sailors are
at the railing.*

HARANA: (*Over the storm*) What is your business, sir?

FRANCISCO: I have a message from Captain Pinzón!

(FRANCISCO *climbs on to the deck.*)

(*Back to his launch*) Stay there! This won't take long!

HARANA: The Admiral, I am afraid, has left word he wishes to see
no one at this time.

FRANCISCO: That does not surprise me. But our message is not
for the Admiral. (*He turns to a sailor who has a bell.*) May I
have that, please? (*He takes the bell and begins to ring it in the
storm.*)

4i

Columbus's cabin and Pinzón's cabin (where PINZÓN *remains alone
at his table).*

   Columbus's cabin – PEDRO *is at the door, listening to the cheers and
shouts coming from the meeting that is taking place with* FRANCISCO
on the deck. SANCHEZ *sits in a corner;* PULGAR *continues to translate;*
COLUMBUS *is still on the bed.*

COLUMBUS: What's he promising them?

(*More shouts.* PEDRO *shakes his head.*)

Tell them – . Tell them, there's a reward!

(*The others turn to him.*)

I have been saving this. Announce to the men that the first to
sight land will receive ten thousand maravedis – a year, for
the rest of his life. (*Pushes* PEDRO.) The first man! Go! Go!

(*He unlocks the door and pushes* PEDRO *out. Then locks it.*)

(*To* PULGAR) We'll pay for it out of the profits. We want

everyone looking, everyone a part of this.
(COLUMBUS *goes back to the bed. A knock at the door.*
SANCHEZ *goes and opens it;* PEDRO *hurries back in.*)
PEDRO: Francisco Pinzón has left. I just saw him – .
COLUMBUS: Did you tell the men about the – .
PEDRO: I didn't have the chance to – .
COLUMBUS: Tell them!!! Tell them about the reward – that'll
make them happy!!
(*He pushes* PEDRO *out again. The storm continues. He slams the
door shut.*)

4j

Columbus's cabin (where all wait) and Pinzón's cabin (where
PINZÓN *sits alone) and Vincente's cabin, the* Niña, *where*
VINCENTE *and* JUAN NIÑOS *enter.*
VINCENTE: (*Entering*) I want a document for everything!
Everything written down. My brothers will remember what
they want to remember.
NIÑOS: I have kept all of their messages.
VINCENTE: (*To himself*) If any of us are fortunate enough to be in
a position to remember. (*Turns to* NIÑOS.) Give me
everything in writing you have. I'll keep it all here. I don't
trust anyone.
(*Short pause.* NIÑOS *is at the window.*)
You understand – that I have not agreed to abandon
Columbus. As the King and Queen's Admiral that would not
be – . I would not do that. All I have done is listen. My men
have listened. Nothing has been agreed.
NIÑOS: This is the position I shall take as well. (*Glancing out of the
window.*) Francisco has left the *Santa Maria.*
VINCENTE: And why my older brother sent Francisco and did not
go himself!! (*Beat.*) Doesn't anyone have any guts?!!!!
(NIÑOS *leaves.* VINCENTE *sits on the table, rubs his eyes – a
man under great strain.*)

4k

All three cabins.
PULGAR: (*Finishing the translation*) This entry, Admiral – it is like

a poem. Worthy of no one less than Marco Polo.

(COLUMBUS *turns and smiles.*)

COLUMBUS: Marco Polo never actually captained a ship, you know.

SANCHEZ: No, I – .

COLUMBUS: All that time, he was never – captain. And he himself did not actually write – . (*He picks up the book of Polo's Travels that is by his bed.*) He dictated that – to someone else. (*He opens the book.*)

SANCHEZ: Who did he – ?

COLUMBUS: (*As he looks through the book*) This was years after he'd returned. He was in prison. (*Looks up.*) This was in Genoa – can you believe the coincidence? In Genoa where I – . As a boy I used to go by the prison.

(*He looks back at the book. When he speaks again it is as almost a mumble: he is reading and speaking at the same time, with the book getting his real attention.*

In his cabin, VINCENTE *picks up his guitar, strums a chord – but it isn't what he wants, so he sets the guitar down and during the rest of the scene he doesn't know where to settle, pours himself a drink, drinks it all down, stands up, sits down, etc.*)

COLUMBUS: (*Mumbling as he reads the book*) He'd been captured – Venice and Genoa: something. I forget why. And another man – though from Pisa, he was in prison and they talked and he wrote it out.

(*The three captains are lost and alone in their own worlds. A knock on Columbus's door.* PULGAR *gets up and opens it.* HARANA *enters.*)

HARANA: (*Entering*) I think it's safer to – stay with friends. No one's really sailing the ship. They're all – just looking.

(PULGAR *shakes his hand as if to say 'Not now.'*)

COLUMBUS: (*Continuing to himself as he reads*) Genoa – same place as where I was born. Now that is an extraordinary coincidence.

(FRANCISCO *enters Pinzón's cabin.* PINZÓN *looks up.*)

FRANCISCO: The crews of both the *Niña* and the *Santa Maria* – (*He breathes deeply*) – await your word – and they shall recognize you as their new Admiral.

(PINZÓN *nods. He closes his eyes.*)

PINZÓN: Well – that took the whole day. (*Beat.*) Now what can
we find to do tomorrow?
(*The storm rages.*)

SCENE 5

Projection: OCTOBER

Columbus's cabin, the Santa Maria. *A few moments before dawn –
the sun will rise during the scene.*

COLUMBUS *and* PULGAR *are at the table, eating the few scraps
that now pass for a meal. A few books are on the table and in a pile on
the floor.* SANCHEZ *and* PEDRO *are both asleep on the floor. A candle
burns on the table. The ship creaks, as it is now basically drifting
along.*

COLUMBUS *takes a book in his hand, looks at it, then tosses it into
the middle of the floor, where a few other books have already been
thrown. He picks up a second book and does the same.*

COLUMBUS: (*With another book*) I'd seen you reading, of course;
you're always – . But I had never before bothered to see
what. I am amazed, Rodrigo. Poetry. (*Tosses the book; takes
another.*) Poetry. (*The same.*) Poetry. (*The same.*) Poetry. I
had no idea. I took you to be a much more level-headed – .
(*Looks at* PULGAR.) I don't know why. Perhaps I never
bothered to really look at you. (*Stares at him.*) You're a lot
more interesting than you seem.
(*Smiles; looks back at a book.*)
Poems, some people say, only confuse a man. They're –
unreal – like dreams. Some days that seems very true. Then
other days . . . (*Beat.*) It's only the dreams that seem real.
(*Looks around his cabin as if at a dream.*)

PULGAR: (*Changing the subject*) I don't imagine the new captain
will wish to keep books – in his cabin. Does Francisco even
read? Do we know? (*Beat.*) If not – maybe he'll need a
secretary.
(*He smiles;* COLUMBUS *looks at him.*)

You or me? (*Bigger smile.*) I know how much you have always
wanted to be a secretary. Especially to a peasant.

COLUMBUS: Maybe then he'll let me sleep in here.

PULGAR: (*Quickly*) Admiral, you know they have agreed already to
that.

COLUMBUS: Everyone's afraid of what the men on deck might do
to me.

PULGAR: That isn't the – .

COLUMBUS: (*With a book*) I loved poetry. Dante and Beatrice – .
(*Stops himself.*) If only what we saw – was like what we read.
The neatness of things. The clarity. Instead, we sit in front of
corpses, with maggots and flies, and try to see – try to draw – a
thigh, a leg and make it beautiful. See it as beautiful. (*Turns to*
PULGAR.) Someone does this. Someone was telling me about
the man who does this. A brilliant draughtsman. I admire
him. (*Beat.*) Without ever even seeing his pictures, I admire
the ambition. The need!
(*On deck a bell has started ringing.*)

PULGAR: I suppose the Pinzóns must be arriving.
(*Beat.* PULGAR *gets up.*)

COLUMBUS: Rodrigo?

PULGAR: I have no regrets. These months on our ship – . I could
not have imagined a better way – to escape.

COLUMBUS: You'll be sorry when you're about to die, and then
you'll hate me too. (*Beat. Turning away.*) I saw land during the
night – did I tell you? I was at the window. I couldn't sleep.
(*A sudden knocking which turns into a pounding on the door.*)

VOICE: (*Off*) Admiral! Admiral, open up!

COLUMBUS: (*Ignoring this*) I know I said that yesterday as well, but
this time . . .

VOICE: (*Pounding*) Admiral! Pedro!

PEDRO: (*Waking*) What's???

PULGAR: (*To* PEDRO) You'd better – . He's going to break it down.

VOICE: (*Off*) Pedro!

PEDRO: (*Getting up*) I'm coming, stop it! I'm coming!
(*The bell has stopped.* PEDRO *opens the door and* HARANA *enters*
with a pail of water.)

HARANA: (*Entering*) I brought the last of the rainwater. I convinced

the men that we should at least have our share.
(*He turns back to* PEDRO, *who is relocking the door.*)
Don't lock it. There's really no need to lock it. Who'd like
water – ?
PULGAR: (*Over this*) Lock it, Pedro.
COLUMBUS: How are the men?
HARANA: The men are – looking. Everyone's hanging over the
railings – .
COLUMBUS: (*To* PULGAR) Because of my reward!!
HARANA: I don't think there's a man who doesn't believe that any
moment – . The Admiral, I have been assured, it is safe for
him to come up on deck.
PEDRO: I don't think he should – .
PULGAR: Lock the door!
COLUMBUS: (*Suddenly standing*) The Admiral will go on deck
whenever he feels like it!!!!
(*Pause.*)
(*To* HARANA) Give me some water.
(HARANA *begins to hand out cups of water.*)
I shall go – wherever I wish to go! There can be no question
of it! And I shall go on deck! But at the moment I am eating.
(*He sits back down, takes a bite and opens a book.*)
(*To* PULGAR) No wonder you wanted to go on such a voyage
– your head was filled with all this poetry – .
HARANA: (*Interrupting*) The Pinzóns are on board.
(*Short pause. No one looks at him.*)
They're talking with some of the men. The new – . Captain
Francisco Pinzón seems – confident. He's brought his trunk.
It's just outside. I'm supposed to bring it – . Into – his cabin.
He asked me. I was pleased about that. (*To* PULGAR) I could
wait if you think – .
COLUMBUS: (*With a book*) This one – the Latin title, it means –
'The New Century'?
(*He turns to* PULGAR, *who nods.* HARANA *does not know what
to do.*)
And you have read it?
(PULGAR *nods.*)
And it was interesting?

PULGAR: Somewhat.

COLUMBUS: Then – it is something to look forward to. (*He carefully sets the book on the table, then looks up.*) To the book, not to the century. Which will be no less ugly than the one we're ending. (*Beat.*) I see no reason why it should be.

HARANA: Then I'll bring in Francisco Pinzón's trunk. (*He goes to the door, unlocks it and goes out.*)

COLUMBUS: (*Continuing his thought*) . . . why it should be, especially given the peasant mind we find ourselves faced with. What we find now before us. These crude, stupid men who are happy to turn everything they touch into a waste. Who are unworthy! Who do not understand – and never will understand – that even had I wished to stop this – . To quit! I could not!!! And if that's a crime – !
(*Stops himself, aware for the first time that* PINZÓN *has entered and probably heard most of this.*)

PINZÓN: The men are fishing. We thought that would be a useful thing to do. And if it rains . . . We're having the barrels ready. We can hope.

COLUMBUS: (*Standing*) We're eating, but if you wish to join us.
(SANCHEZ *groans in his sleep.*)
(*To* SANCHEZ) Get up! (*To* PEDRO) Get him up! Admiral Martín Pinzón has come to see us!!
(PEDRO *shakes* SANCHEZ.)

SANCHEZ: What – ?

PEDRO: Sh-sh!

PINZÓN: (*Over this*) I'm not hungry. Thank you. (*Beat.*) And – I apologize for not having accepted – .

COLUMBUS: I'll get him up! (*Goes to* SANCHEZ *and kicks him.*)
Wake up – this is an honour!

PINZÓN: For not having accepted – .

COLUMBUS: He's awake. What?

PINZÓN: Accepted – your generous offers before. My – loss.
(*An awkward pause. No one knows what to say.* PINZÓN *looks at the pile of books in the middle of the floor.*)

PULGAR: My books. I didn't know whether to leave them for your brother.

PINZÓN: Francisco – rarely reads, I think.

COLUMBUS: What a surprise.

PINZÓN: Your books are your books, Señor Pulgar. Do with them as you choose. No one wishes to make this any more difficult than it is.

COLUMBUS: Then leave us alone. And get off my ship!!

PINZÓN: It was not my idea, Admiral! (*Beat.*) And Francisco insists on all the trappings of being the captain of the *Santa Maria*! So – ! (*Beat.*) I am very sorry. I have made him agree, of course, that you be allowed to keep most of your things – . Wherever. Nothing you need will be moved. You will sleep in here as well.

COLUMBUS: (*To* SANCHEZ) Get up! Let me see how the floor feels!

(FRANCISCO *enters, talking.*)

FRANCISCO: The men seem – relieved. That was my impression. We had a good talk.

(VINCENTE, QUINTEROS *and* JUAN NIÑOS *are behind him.*)

COLUMBUS: I shall speak to the men as well!!

FRANCISCO: So speak to them!!! Who's been stopping you?!! They haven't even seen your face in a week!!

(*Short pause. The others look at each other, surprised at the outburst. A sense of discomfort.* HARANA *enters, dragging in a trunk. All watch him for a moment.*)

COLUMBUS: (*Quietly*) I will speak to them. As soon as I . . . (*Gestures towards his food. He eats.*) I'm eating.

FRANCISCO: God only knows what you could say to them.

PINZÓN: Francisco, please. You promised you wouldn't – .

FRANCISCO: I hadn't realized how I'd feel once I saw his face.

(COLUMBUS *looks down and eats.*)

Look at him. I've half a mind to let you finish eating and then drag you outside. What could you say to them? What can you say to any of us?! (*He suddenly and violently knocks the food out of* COLUMBUS's *hands.*)

PINZÓN: Francisco – !

VINCENTE: I do not agree with this. I do not agree with Francisco being made captain.

PINZÓN: (*Shocked*) You didn't say anything when we discussed – .

III

VINCENTE: He pushed to be made captain. I want that understood – .

PINZÓN: That was not the reason – . I asked Francisco!

VINCENTE: That is the first I've heard you say it was you – . Why didn't you talk with me?! I'm the captain of the – !

PINZÓN: I assumed you'd agree that Francisco – .

VINCENTE: Juan Niños is a much more obvious choice!

NIÑOS: I wouldn't want – .

VINCENTE: Or Quinteros or – . They're older, they're – .

PINZÓN: I didn't ask you!

VINCENTE: I have just realized that!

PINZÓN: Francisco is the new captain of the *Santa Maria*!! This is my order – as the admiral of this fleet!!! (*Stops himself.*) As the commander of – . I haven't given myself the title – . Of Admiral.

(*In the distance a cannon is fired.*)

COLUMBUS: (*To* PULGAR) What's – ?

PULGAR: Perhaps they're shooting at the birds now with cannon-balls.

FRANCISCO: Señor Columbus, would you kindly leave my cabin? I shall see that space is provided on deck – .

PULGAR: (*Over this*) That's not what we agreed!

QUINTEROS: (*To* PINZÓN, *at the same time*) Sir, we agreed to let the Admiral stay – .

PINZÓN: Francisco, we had a deal! Columbus would not be asked to vacate – .

QUINTEROS: (*Over this*) I would not have participated – !

FRANCISCO: (*At the same time*) He's a criminal! Let the men do to him whatever they wish – !

VINCENTE: (*At the same time*) I will not allow – !

PINZÓN: (*Yells*) He stays!!!!! Do you understand?!!!!

(*Short pause.*)

FRANCISCO: (*To* COLUMBUS) Stay. (*Beat.*) But you sleep on the floor.

COLUMBUS: I like that spot there, I think.

FRANCISCO: (*Ignoring this, to his brothers*) And that is *my* decision!

(*Beat.*)

VINCENTE: I had hoped we could have handled this with some dignity.

FRANCISCO: (*To* COLUMBUS) Why do they defend you? This is what I can't – . It makes no sense to me. Please, I beg you – go and talk to the men. This I wish to witness. Look in their eyes and see how they hate you for – for what you have done to us! For this tragedy! For our misery! For your crimes!!

VINCENTE: (*To* PINZÓN) I do not wish to be a party to – .

FRANCISCO: (*Turns to* VINCENTE) Have some guts, brother!

VINCENTE: This is not a trial. And if it were, who made you – ?

FRANCISCO: Because of him we're – !!

PINZÓN: (*At the same time*) I blame myself too!

FRANCISCO: As you should! As I do!

VINCENTE: No one ever forced you to come – .

FRANCISCO: I believed what I was told. What my older brothers told me. If that is a crime, then . . .

PINZÓN: Here isn't the place – .

VINCENTE: He's completely panicked. I wish to petition the fleet to remove Francisco as captain. His behaviour, it should be obvious – .

FRANCISCO: Get off my ship!!!

PINZÓN: Stop this!!

FRANCISCO: I wish to petition Vincente be removed – !!

VINCENTE: And I propose that Señor Quinteros be made – !!

QUINTEROS: I do not wish to – !

VINCENTE: (*Yelling*) He's panicked! He's panicked!!

FRANCISCO: (*Yelling at the same time*) To hell with you! Hell with you!

(*The argument has degenerated into two brothers standing face to face and yelling names at each other.*)

PINZÓN: (*Screams*) Stop it!! Stop it!!

(*They stop, out of breath – as is* PINZÓN. COLUMBUS *has watched all this with amusement.*)

This is not how to solve – ! We have a responsibility to those men up there! (*Beat.*) How low can we sink? How small? And in front of the Admiral.

(*He breathes very deeply, holds his head in his hands – he doesn't know what to do. An out-of-breath* SAILOR *hurries in.*)

SALOR: Sirs!
PINZÓN: (*To his brothers*) We solve nothing by – !
SAILORS: Sirs!
PINZÓN: (*Quickly*) What?!
    (*Beat.*)
SAILOR: Land.
    (*They all turn to the* SAILOR. *Beat.*)

SCENE 6

Projection: A FEW HOURS LATER

Columbus's cabin, the Santa Maria. *The cabin is packed with the officers of all three ships –* NIÑOS, LUIS DE TORRES, HARANA, SANCHEZ, PINZÓN, FRANCISCO, VINCENTE, PULGAR, QUINTEROS *and many more – as well as* PEDRO *and* COLUMBUS, *who is struggling to get his armour breastplate on.*

A sense of the room being very overcrowded, people forced against each other; difficult to move one's arms, etc. They are there for a toast, before COLUMBUS *speaks to the men on deck.* PEDRO *has a bottle that he pours from –* NIÑOS *is trying to get a little more out of the bottle. Everyone is talking.*

COLUMBUS: (*Struggling with the armour*) Out of the jaws of defeat!
    (*He laughs.*)
QUINTEROS: (*To* NIÑOS) Careful, that was all that we were hoarding.
LUIS: (*Holding up another bottle*) We were hoarding this!
    (*Laughter.*)
COLUMBUS: (*Continuing*) So to speak.
    (*Drums in the distance, from the land.*)
HARANA: Listen – .
    (*Everyone hushes everyone. They listen.*)
COLUMBUS: They're going to be talking about us.
QUINTEROS: Bet they're not as happy to see us as we are to see – .
COLUMBUS: I'm sure they're very happy.
    (*A cannon shot outside.*)
SANCHEZ: What was – ?

VINCENTE: I told my men – if they wish to celebrate . . .

QUINTEROS: And scare the hell out of those Japanese!

HARANA: They looked scared enough already.

COLUMBUS: (*Still struggling with the armour*) I know it's hot in here. There's too many people! (*Smiles.*) But I wanted to do this before addressing the men. I thought – . Just us officers – . How long will that take, Pedro?

PEDRO: I'm just about finished. (*He continues to pour.*)

PINZÓN: Did anyone else notice the oars? The carved handles of the oars some of them – .

COLUMBUS: I didn't notice.

SANCHEZ: They seem a docile group – the natives – .

COLUMBUS: A couple of men with a gun – one gun, that's all it would take – and you could – .

OFFICER: (*To someone in the back*) Stop pushing!

COLUMBUS: You could – whatever. One gun!

LUIS: If I heard it right – their language has some affinity with – Hebrew.

PULGAR: Could you understand – ?

LUIS: I need to hear more, but – .

PULGAR: What words were like Hebrew?

LUIS: It's an impression. A feeling I have.

COLUMBUS: (*Stops getting his armour on; tries to get their attention*) I'm sorry it's so close in here. But please – does everyone now have a glass – ?

PEDRO: The bottles are empty!

COLUMBUS: Then everyone's – . We're ready. I simply wanted to say – to each and – .

MAN AT THE BACK: Admiral, we can't hear!

COLUMBUS: To all of you!! Better? To all of you, my heartfelt congratulations! It has been a long journey for us. But one made, I proudly add, with courage and belief – by some of us. By others – with doubt, questioning, fear, panic and recrimination. (*Beat.*) But I wish to blame no one. Not now. Not yet. Let history decide who was right. And who was wrong. Is that all right with you, Francisco? Where's – ? (*Looks around.*) There he is. (COLUMBUS *smiles.*) I don't mean to embarrass anyone. Gentlemen, by this achievement today, we tell the world who we are. Justify what we have done, declare who we have become. This accomplishment, this fact is now ours – we have sailed these three ships across the Ocean Sea to Japan!!!

(*Applause and cheers.*)

We began this voyage and I said we would all have the opportunity of being reborn. I believe that is just what has happened today. No less than that. (*Beat.*)

As we look back over these weeks, months at sea, we may recall the trials, the confusions and the discomforts that beset us along the way. But as men of the world, we know that these are but typical of a venture such as ours. We could have expected nothing less. One could imagine much much worse. I'm sweating in this. (*Moves his breastplate around.*) But we persevered, I led – and you followed. I owe you my deepest gratitude for showing such confidence in me, a foreigner. I look at your faces now and the pride you are feeling; the pride in yourselves. In your fellow officers. In your crews. In your Admiral. (*Beat.*) I thank you. And now, everyone please raise your – cups or whatever you've been given, and let us drink to those who sanctioned this voyage and chartered its way. (*Beat.*) To the Queen and King of Spain!!

ALL: To the Queen and King of Spain!

(*They drink. Short pause. No one knows what else to do.*)

COLUMBUS: (*Finally*) That's all. I don't have anything else to say! It's stuffy in here – . (*To one officer*) I wasn't very – . Hopefully I'll be a little more articulate with the crews – .

(*A number of the officers take the hint and say how wonderful his toast was, etc.*)

VINCENTE: (*Over this*) Admiral, before we go – .

PINZÓN: Quiet, everyone! Please!

(*Everyone quietens down.*)

SANCHEZ: Listen – you can still hear the drums.

VINCENTE: The young sailor who first sighted land is on deck. I brought him on board. He's waiting. I think everyone should meet – . He's become quite the celebrity among the men on my ship. Ten thousand maravedis for life and who wouldn't!

(*Laughter.*)

NIÑOS: Bring him in – !

QUINTEROS: The officers should honour – !

PINZÓN: Rodrigo de Triana, he's from Lepe!

PULGAR: (*Feigning shock*) He's not a relative!

(*Laughter.*)

VINCENTE: I'll get him.

COLUMBUS: Wait.

(VINCENTE *stops. Beat.* COLUMBUS *clears his throat.*)

Before you do. I was going to wait on this myself, but I now see that I mustn't. (*Beat.*) I believe Señor Pulgar can correct the misunderstanding that seems to have arisen about this – . (*Gestures in the air.*) The reward.

PULGAR: (*Confused*) What are you – ?

COLUMBUS: Pulgar and I – . On second thought, last night it was only me who was looking out. You were asleep. I was looking out – just there, at that window.

(*Some turn to see the window.*)

I should show you. (*He pushes through the crowd.*) Excuse me. Could I get through – . Thank you. Hello, I didn't see you. What a day, isn't it? (*He reaches the window.*) Here. This is where I stood when I first sighted land last night.

(*Beat.*)

VINCENTE: In the night – ?

COLUMBUS: There was a light. There must have been fires. (*Shrugs.*) I stood right here.

(*No one says anything.*)

And I told Pulgar this – just this morning. Didn't I?

PULGAR: Yes, you mentioned – .

COLUMBUS: And I suspect my steward, Pedro, could also be my witness, should I need witnesses – which I don't. (*Beat. Looks out.*) Just a light. Of course I do not wish to take anything away from a sailor, but what is right is right. The man would not want my charity; he'd want to know he'd earned the ten thousand maravedis. Which of course for the sake of truth – and history – I am forced now by honour to claim for myself.

(*Silence.*)

Anyone have any problem with that?
(*Short pause, then everyone starts to leave, ignoring Columbus's question.*)

PINZÓN: (*To whomever is next to him*) I'd like to have a chance here to take a look at our hull. We've been taking in some water.

NIÑOS: (*To* VINCENTE) Who's going to talk to the sailor – ?

VINCENTE: (*Turns to* COLUMBUS, *ignoring* NIÑOS) Admiral, some of the men have asked – about the native women. What we – . The rules. What they are allowed.

PINZÓN: We've all seen that the women are – .

QUINTEROS: Undressed!
(*He laughs, no one else does. Beat.*)

COLUMBUS: Well – there certainly shall be no marrying!
(*Beat. The others take this for a joke and laugh, and then* COLUMBUS *laughs. Almost everyone has left;* VINCENTE, *at the door, turns back.*)

VINCENTE: And you are sure, sir – that this is – Japan?
(*Beat. Then a huge laugh from others behind him and those leaving;* COLUMBUS *smiles. The joke is passed along outside to those who didn't hear it, and they laugh.*)
I suppose that was a stupid question.
(*Laughter continues off.* VINCENTE *leaves.* PEDRO *too has left with the cups.* COLUMBUS *and* PULGAR *are alone.* COLUMBUS *laughs to himself at the joke, then continues to struggle with the armour.*)

COLUMBUS: I hate this thing; it makes me sweat like . . . (*To* PULGAR, *without looking at him.*) Pull on this strap, will you? (PULGAR *doesn't move.*) Pull on the – (*Turns to* PULGAR.) Did you hear me?
(PULGAR *gets up and goes and helps him.*)
What do you think? Should I have attacked Francisco? At first I thought I would, but – .

PULGAR: I thought that was a mistake.

COLUMBUS: Generosity, Rodrigo, is sometimes the best strategy. We still need to get home. I have forgotten nothing.

PULGAR: I meant – about the sailor who sighted – .
I thought that was a mistake.

COLUMBUS (*Not looking at him*) Ten thousand maravedis a year is
a lot of money. And I did see land first. You are my witness.
Or are you contradicting – ?
PULGAR: You have said you've seen land every day for the last
two weeks.
COLUMBUS: And I saw it today too. So? (*Turns to* PULGAR.) I
don't understand, Rodrigo. Why is that bothering you?
PULGAR: The men – won't they resent – ?
COLUMBUS: They'll forget it. They now have other things to
think about. (*Smiles. His smile grows as he remembers his
'joke'.*) 'There won't be any marrying!'
(*He laughs,* PULGAR *doesn't.* PEDRO *enters.*)
PEDRO: The men are waiting.
COLUMBUS: As soon as I get this on – .
PEDRO: Let me help – .
COLUMBUS: Rodrigo's helping me.
PEDRO: (*Nods*) The natives – hear the drumming? They're in
their boats. Hundreds of them, on their way out here. It
looks like they're really not scared of us.
COLUMBUS: I'll be right there.
(PEDRO *nods and leaves, leaving the door open. The drumming
is louder now.*)
Listen. (*Smiles. Listens to the drumming.*) Exciting, isn't it?
PULGAR: Yes. It is exciting. (*Beat.*) What you did to the sailor, it
seemed – unnecessary, that's all.
COLUMBUS: (*Suddenly turns on* PULGAR *with a rage*) Ten thousand
maravedis is not unnecessary!! Not to me! Not if you've been
poor!!! And I'm not going to defend myself to you!!
PULGAR: (*Suddenly and passionately stands up to him*) Just when
you were proven right!
COLUMBUS: (*Over this – warning him to stop*) Pulgar!!
PULGAR: (*Continuing fighting back*) We're here, across the sea!
The scholars were wrong! You were right!! Today I've
looked at you so differently!!!
(*He holds his head, tries not to cry. Pause.* COLUMBUS *looks at
him, then sighs.*)
COLUMBUS: If that sailor had been Admiral and I had been the
sailor, he would have done the same to me. I promise you.

(*Beat.*) But your point is well taken. I won't do it again. Whatever it is you say I did, I won't do it again. (*Beat.*) How's that?

(PINZÓN *is at the doorway, and startles both of them.*)

PINZÓN: The men are calling for you, Admiral.

(COLUMBUS *nods at* PINZÓN, *who leaves. From the deck now, along with the drumming, one hears the crew beginning to call out for the Admiral.* COLUMBUS *finishes putting the armour on.*)

COLUMBUS: There. (*Turns to* PULGAR, *then pats him on the shoulder.*) This is a great day. Let us enjoy it.

(COLUMBUS *takes his sword and goes to the door, stops, turns back to* PULGAR.)

(*Shouts*) Look at all we've done, Rodrigo!! (*He smiles.*) It's incredible! What we've done. (*Beat.*) We made it. We're here.

(*He goes out. Deafening cheers from the deck as* COLUMBUS *appears before the crew – this heard through the open door. After a moment,* PULGAR *follows through the door. In the distance, the huge sail of the* Santa Maria *with its giant red cross; it now has many holes, rips, and stains.*)